QUICKIES ⚥

QUICKIES

Fascinating Facts About the Facts of Life

DON VOORHEES

CITADEL PRESS
Kensington Publishing Corp.
www.kensingtonbooks.com

CITADEL PRESS BOOKS are published by

Kensington Publishing Corp.
850 Third Avenue
New York, NY 10022

All Kensington titles, imprints, and distributed lines are available at special quantity discounts for bulk purchases for sales promotions, premiums, fund-raising, educational, or institutional use. Special book excerpts or customized printings can also be created to fit specific needs. For details, write or phone the office of the Kensington special sales manager: Kensington Publishing Corp., 850 Third Avenue, New York, NY 10022, Attn: Special Sales Department; phone 1-800-221-2647.

First printing: April 2004

10 9 8 7 6 5 4 3 2

Printed in the United States of America

Library of Congress Control Number: 2003110768

ISBN 0-8065-2550-9

CONTENTS

QUICKIES ⚥

CHAPTER ONE

Man's Best Friend

How long does it take a guy to get an erection?

Not too long, as you probably already know. Guys can be ready for action in the blink of an eye—well, almost. The average man can get it up in a mere ten seconds.

Once he actually gets down to the business of intercourse, he will thrust an average of 60 to 120 times. Most men will ejaculate within two to three minutes' time. For the amount of thought and money spent on sex, you'd think it would last a little longer.

Well, it does last a little longer for women. Famed sex researcher Alfred Kinsey found that a female will climax in about four minutes when masturbating, but it can take anywhere from ten to twenty minutes during intercourse. If you do the math, it doesn't seem like there would be many couples having simultaneous orgasms out there.

So what is the average length of an erect penis?

This is one of those questions that always seems to get a different answer. Alfred Kinsey conducted a study of penile length in the mid-1940s. He came up with an average erect penis length of around 6.3 inches. Since that time, many men have felt shortchanged. Those of you who don't measure up, take heart. A new study has lowered the bar, so to speak.

The Kinsey study was somewhat flawed. He gave men stamped postcards, and instructed them to hold the card up to the base of their members, mark off the length, and pop it in the mail. Done privately, these measurements may have been taken haphazardly, with little uniformity in the measuring procedure—not to mention the possibility that some men may have been a little overly generous.

A more scientifically reliable survey was recently conducted by the folks at Lifestyle Condoms Company. During spring break of 2001, in Cancun, Mexico, they rounded up approximately three hundred college-age guys outside Daddy Rock nightclub. In a private tent, they gave them porn magazines to put them in the mood and had a doctor and two nurses size them up. (In case you were wondering, you measure from where the top of the penis meets the body, while holding it straight out, perpendicular to the torso). The results? The average erect penis measures 5.87 inches—about the size of a Butterfinger candy bar. This is about a half an inch shorter than found in previous studies, including Kinsey's. Two-thirds of the men ranged from 5.1 to 6.2 inches. Average penis circumference was about 4.9 inches.

What is a "micropenis"?

As you probably guessed from the name, this is the term for a very small penis. There are numerous records of men unfortunate enough to possess a penis no longer than one centimeter in length when fully erect. These men are good candidates for extension surgery, which can add a couple of inches. (See following question.)

Can you have your penis lengthened?

Yes, you *can* have your penis lengthened. In an operation called phalloplasty, the suspensory ligaments on top of the penis are cut, allowing the penis to extend to a greater length—between three-eighths of an inch and two inches. The suspensory ligaments hold the penis to the lower abdomen. When they are cut, the penis falls forward, looking longer. The lower portion of the penis that was held in the abdomen is now hanging outside. As such, some of the upward angle of your erection is lost.

The penis can also be surgically lengthened using pieces of skin taken from the groin. This is considered a somewhat drastic measure, however, performed in rather extreme cases where the man's penis is much smaller than average.

The girth of the penis can also be enhanced by about two inches. Fat can be suctioned from other parts of the body and injected into the supposedly inadequate member. The result is a fatter but mushier erection. The procedure may have to be repeated periodically to retain the added girth. Both procedures can be performed in under an hour using local anesthesia for around $6,000. Close to 6,000 American men have their members lengthened each year.

While desperate men do have some limited options, women still corner the market in surgical enhancement.

What is "scrotal infusion"?

The scrotum is an enclosed sac. It is possible to inject fluids into the sac and cause it to greatly swell. This is also known as "ballooning," since the engorged scrotum resembles a water balloon. This painless, if bizarre, practice has one side effect that makes it popular among a select few—within twenty-four hours the fluid in the scrotum filters into the penis, expanding it to a quite prodigious girth. It's NOT advisable to try such foolishness.

What are the advantages of a large penis?

Surprisingly, *only* sixty percent of women say they really care about the size of a man's penis, according to a poll by *Complete Woman* magazine. Compared to much of the animal kingdom, the human penis is rather thick in relation to its length. It is the thickness of the penis that gives the woman pleasure. A thick penis distends the muscles of the lower vagina. This pulls on the hood of the clitoris, causing friction and stimulation. A longer penis is better, however, at promoting conception. It pushes the sperm deeper, making the trip for the egg that much shorter.

It may interest you to know that not all peoples have admired a large penis. It is said that the ancient Greeks preferred a small firm one, believing that the sperm would have a shorter path to travel into the woman and would thus be more potent.

Do men with big feet have big penises?

The size of a man's feet or hands has no relation to his penis size. The best indicator of the size of a man's penis is the size of his father's penis. Unlike many other traits, penis size seems to be inherited directly from Dad. If father is well hung, so should be junior. However, this bit of information won't really help you size up a prospective mate, unless you can get a peek at his dad.

When sizing up a penis, you really can't go by its length when flaccid. Certain studies have indicated that men with smaller penises experience a greater increase in size from the flaccid to the erect state. Apparently, the larger the flaccid penis, the less it will increase in size during an erection. A small penis may actually double in size when excited. A good way to tell, if you can manage it, is to take the flaccid penis and stretch it out. This will give you a fair indication of its length when fully erect.

One more thing. Don't try to judge a guy's true size until he reaches at least eighteen years of age. Not only would it be illegal, but the average boy's penis does not reach its full size until that time.

What is the most embarrassing male medical condition?

You might think that it would be impotence or premature ejaculation. Think again. While these two conditions are quite embarrassing, they are only revealed to the most intimate people in a man's life. A condition known as "priapism," however, is there for all to see. It's an affliction where a man gets a spontaneous, long-lasting erection that he has no control over. This is sure to get a few chuckles at the office as well as at the beach. The erection can also be very painful and its treatment requires draining the blood away from the base of the enlarged penis through tiny incisions.

The word priapism comes from Greek mythology. Aphrodite, the Greek goddess of love and sex, had a son named Priapus, the Greek god of fertility, who was blessed (or cursed) with a perpetual erection.

Can an erection break?

Talk about painful. This freak occurrence must rank pretty high on the male pain-threshold scale. "Hard" as it may be to believe, it is possible to break an erection. There are about twenty-five reported cases a year. The most common cause is reportedly as a result of overenthusiastic masturbation. Another way to break your penis is thrusting too hard during intercourse and inadvertently missing the vagina, causing it to crash into the woman's pubic bone or perineum. People have even broken an erection by rolling over on it, bumping it into a bedpost or night table, or forcing it into a pair of pants.

How do you know if you have broken your penis? The symptoms will be immediate and severe, marked by unbearable pain and a swelling of the penis circumference by three to four times its normal size. A doctor should be consulted immediately. An operation to repair the torn tissue may be required, as well as a draining of excess blood. So be careful in bed, guys!

Are you a dribbler or a shooter?

If you are a basketball player you are both, but that's not what we're talking about here. Most men either shoot their semen out in a spurt or have it dribble out. If you are a dribbler, you'll probably always be one. Some sex therapists, however, claim there is an exercise you can do to strengthen the "shooting" muscle—the pubococcygeus. This is the muscle you use to squeeze out the last few drops of urine. To strengthen it, contract it ten times, holding each contraction for five seconds, three or four times a day. These exercises are known as "kegels." They may or may not improve your shooting ability, but could help to intensify your orgasms. (For more on kegels, see pages 120–121.)

How fast does semen travel when ejaculated?

The things that we think of while trying to control our orgasms. . . .

If this one ever crossed your mind, you will be interested to learn that semen can reach up to twenty-eight mph when ejaculated. A really good shot can go about two or three feet and can contain up to 787 million sperm! That's enough sperm to fertilize every woman in Europe. The number of sperm, and the distance traveled, for that matter, has to do with the number of recent orgasms a man has had. Each successive ejaculation contains less sperm and probably travels less distance.

Why do some men have bent penises?

A penis is like a face—no two are exactly the same. Most are straight, but some can curve slightly off to one side, which is okay. However, there is a condition known as Peyronie's disease, where a normal straight erection will begin to develop a pronounced curve to one side.

Urologists believe the cause of the curve is from some kind of trauma. Even a minor injury can result in the formation of scar tissue that bends the erect penis to the side. Usually the penis will straighten somewhat after several months. Unless the condition is painful or interferes with your sex life, you should not worry about it. For serious cases, surgery can be performed that will straighten out your member, but also shorten it.

Why do men have erections in their sleep?

One theory, put forth by Boston University urologist, Dr. Irwin Goldstein, is that nocturnal erections supply needed blood to the penis, thus replenishing its oxygen supply. Studies have shown that a flaccid penis is probably the most oxygen-deprived organ in the body. Without the occasional erection, the cells in the penis could die from a lack of oxygen. Nighttime erections supply enough oxygen to keep the penis healthy throughout the day. The more immediately obvious causes of sleep erections are having sexual dreams and the inadvertent rubbing of the penis against the bedding. The latter may sometimes cause the former to occur, and vice versa.

Can science grow you a new penis?

If your penis is damaged or nonfunctional, the branch of science that may one day be able to help you is called tissue engineering. The technology already exists to grow replacement genitals in a lab for animals. Healthy tissue is biopsied from the patient and grown in a liquid medium. The liquid tissue culture is then squirted onto and injected into a biodegradable mold of the desired organ's shape and size; a penis, a clitoris, or whatever. The tissue will grow to the dimensions of the template. Presto! New genitals.

Can a man have more than one penis?

Does this sound like a curse, or a blessing? Either way, the phenomenon is called "diphallasparatus," and involves having two penises. And yes, it is a curse. These poor men are sterile. Only a few dozen of these cases have ever been substantiated. The two penises can be one on top of the other, although side by side is the more common positioning. They are the same size and urine may pass through either one, or both.

Can a man have more than two testicles?

You should have figured out by now that the human body is capable of almost any kind of growth anomaly, including multiple testicles, which is known as "polyorchidism." This is another extremely rare condition. Most sufferers have three testicles, although four or five have been known to occur.

How big can testicles get?

Unlike penises, which can vary somewhat in size, testicles are all generally in the same size "ball"park (sorry)—4 to 4½ centimeters long and 2 to 2½ centimeters broad. The largest are around 5 centimeters long. However, there are rare conditions, such as elephantiasis, a disease caused by parasitic worms that block the lymph glands. For people with this condition, the testicles can swell to the size of footballs! One unfortunate fellow had a pair weighing 150 pounds and needed a wheelbarrow to get around! Happily, the drug diethylcarbamazine can be administered to kill the parasites and reduce the swelling.

Is one testicle supposed to be larger than the other?

Most men have one testicle that is larger than the other. Eighty percent of the time, the left one hangs lower than the right. This is perfectly normal and is no cause for concern. In right-handed men, the left testicle tends to be lower. In left-handed men, it's usually the right. One reason the testicles may be offset is that this prevents them from banging against one another when moving about.

Are men with bigger testicles more promiscuous?

Scientists have noticed that gorillas, who have relatively small testicles, are much more monogamous than their randy relatives the chimpanzees, whose testicles are larger. This caused evolutionary biologist Robin Baker to wonder if there is any correlation in humans, between the size of a man's testicles and how promiscuous he is.

Baker conducted a written survey of eighty male college students and found that the bigger a man's testicles were, the more active his sex life and the more likely he was to have cheated on his partner. His conclusion was that "bad boys have big balls." However, his sample size was small and he didn't measure their testicles himself, so the results may be skewed. Perhaps bad boys lie about the size of their balls, or the amount of sex they are having. But if you want to play it safe, ladies, look for a mate with small testicles, just in case.

What are "blue balls"?

For you women readers out there who have no idea what a pain "blue balls" can be, imagine severe menstrual cramps, only swinging between your legs. Actually, the pain of blue balls is more comparable to a tension headache, and it has a similar cause.

Blue balls is a common enough problem that can occur for a man, usually a younger one, who has become very sexually aroused for a period of time, but for one reason or another did not ejaculate. This can happen after heavy petting sessions or foreplay, when the sex act is not consummated.

The source of the discomfort is vasocongestive pressure in the penis and testicles. As a result of all the blood being pumped into the genitals during sexual arousal, the scrotum can turn a purplish or bluish color (hence the term "blue balls") and the testicles can enlarge by 50 percent or more. Muscular tension and constricted blood vessels will maintain this pressure until it is released at orgasm. However, if a man does not ejaculate, the blood will slowly flow out of the narrowed blood vessels, causing discomfort in the testes. The best cure for blue balls is either masturbation or convincing your partner to accommodate you.

Why does a cold shower cause a man's genitals to shrivel up?

Perhaps nothing is more embarrassing to a man than to be spied after emerging from a cold shower. Even the most well-endowed male will notice a sudden, rather unflattering change in his anatomy. The reason for this curious phenomenon is easily explained.

Each testicle is suspended on a muscle, called a cremaster, that regulates the way it hangs. When the cremaster muscles are relaxed, the testicles hang low in the scrotum. When they contract, the testicles are pulled up, sometimes into the inguinal area of the lower abdomen. This phenomenon of the disappearing testicles occurs during ejaculation or in response to cold or fear. Extreme exhaustion, fatigue, or excitement can have the same result.

(Check out your member next time your team scores a touchdown in a big game.)

The penis itself shrinks because the cold water contracts the blood vessels that supply and inflate it with blood. The shrinkage can be so great that it's almost funny—at least when it happens to an overly sensitive male. (Such was the case in a hilarious episode of the TV sitcom *Seinfeld*, when the character George had a most embarrassing encounter.) You ladies may think it's cute, but if a woman's breasts shrank two sizes in cold water, you'd probably never set foot in a pool again!

What happens when a man has an orgasm?

There are several steps involved in the often far too short chain of events of the male orgasm. First the penis swells to its fully erect size and the head (glans) darkens in color, from the blood inside. Next, the opening of the urethra (the hole at the tip of the penis) widens and fluid from the Cowper's glands moistens the tip of the glans, providing some lubrication. The testicles swell to almost double their normal size and rotate and rise up close to the body. The man's heart rate almost doubles, as does his blood pressure, and his rate of breathing can also triple. The muscles of the body all become tense, the toes curl, the feet arch, and the hands grasp. The face becomes contorted, and any number of unusual sounds may emanate from the mouth. The nipples harden and the skin on the face, chest, and buttocks may redden (sex flush). The tissues of the nose swell, making breathing more difficult. As soon as ejaculation is finished, the man breaks into a sweat. Then, a feeling of total relaxation is achieved, and sleep can easily follow. The end.

How many sperm does a man produce in a day?

Talk about mass production—a man makes about 50,000 sperm every minute of his adult life. Do the math. That's 3,000,000 per hour, 72,000,000 a day. The average ejaculation sends hundreds of millions of these little guys on their merry way.

Why so many sperm? Because not many will ever reach their final destination, assuming they are shot out into a woman's vagina. Around ten percent could be abnormal, so they are out of contention right off the bat. For the rest, its a race to the egg.

It's a tough world out there (in there) and the journey is long and arduous. The seminal fluid offers some protection for the early stages of the migration. Being alkaline, it helps shield the sperm from the acidic environment of the vagina. The semen also has some antibacterial properties, just in case. However, it's a matter of sheer physical stamina that determines the winner of this sperm marathon.

A good sense of direction is crucial. In the trip from the vagina, through the uterus and up the oviduct, many sperm will swim sideways or backward. Others will tire. Some will pick the wrong oviduct (only one has an egg). Swimming at the rate of a few millimeters a minute, it's a long haul. However, the little guys don't have to swim all the way from the cervix to the upper fallopian, since the tubes are lined with tiny hairs (cilia) that move in a wavelike motion to push them along their way.

Once the egg is within sight, as it were, the hundred or so remaining sperm make a final mad dash for the finish line. Upon reaching the outer wall of the egg, the lucky few release a chemical to make a hole and gain entry. Only the head of the sperm will get through the outer wall. Now this swimming head must breach the inner egg wall to reach the final prize—the nucleus.

Only one sperm will be able to fuse its nucleus with that of the egg. Fusion combines their DNA—twenty-three chromosomes of the sperm with the twenty-three chromosomes of the egg. Sexual reproduction has thus been accomplished, with the conception of a child with half maternal DNA and half paternal DNA.

Do you ever notice jelly-like lumps in your semen?

If you are the kind of guy who takes note of such things, your semen can "come" in a wide range of colors and consistencies. Both thick and thin are normal. Sometimes you may notice thick,

gelatinous globs in your ejaculate. This is quite normal, as glob-
ules of enzymes and proteins form in your prostate gland if you
haven't ejaculated recently.

Your semen can also range in color from almost clear, to different shades of white, yellow, or gray. Like the lumps, yellow semen
may be noticed after a short break in sexual activity. Various medicines can also change its color.

Semen comes out as a liquid and quickly turns to a gel. After a
period of several minutes it will reliquify. The biological reason
for the transformation to a gel state is to prevent the sperm from
dripping out of the vagina. The reliquification helps the sperm to
swim upstream to the fallopian tubes. Enzymes in the semen are
responsible for this change of state.

How many calories are there in semen?

Many of you women watch your weight and count every calorie. Even the difference between a teaspoon of sugar and a packet
of Equal seems important. Well, what about sperm? You practitioners of fellatio out there will be glad to learn that a little semen
shouldn't go right to your hips.

Semen is composed of seminal fluid and spermatozoa. The
sperm, which is made in the testicles, makes up about three percent of the average ejaculate. The seminal fluid makes up the
other ninety-seven percent and is produced in the prostate and
the seminal vesicles. The first spurt of an ejaculation contains the
most sperm. The seminal fluid is squirted behind the sperm as it
passes the prostate gland. Semen contains very small amounts of
more than thirty chemicals, including ascorbic acid, blood group
antigens, calcium, chlorine, cholesterol, citric acid, creatine, DNA,
fructose, glutathione, hyaluronidase, inositol, lactic acid, nitrogen,
phosphorus, potassium, pyruvic acid, sodium, sorbitol, spermi-
dine, spermine, urea, uric acid, vitamin B12, and zinc. This sounds
like a lot of good stuff, but semen's nutritional value is about nil,
although it does nourish the sperm while in the vagina.

As far as calories go, the average one teaspoon of ejaculate contains only a few calories, whereas the average lovemaking session can burn off something in the neighborhood of 100 calories. So, if you're a spitter, you can't use calorie counting as an excuse anymore.

What can affect the taste of semen?

Some people seem to like the taste of semen, at least during the passion of fellatio, while others detest it. Did you know that the taste of semen can change according to several different factors? A man's diet and state of health are two keys to the way his semen will taste. Vegetarians who eat lots of celery tend to have mild semen (as will a man who has ejaculated several times in the past couple of days), while red meat, asparagus, broccoli, and spinach produce sharp-tasting semen. The more sperm in the ejaculate, the sharper in taste it will be.

Smoking cigarettes and pot or drinking alcohol make the semen bitter. A diabetic's semen is usually sweet. Combinations of these factors can produce a moderate taste. It is said that a vasectomy imparts a milder taste to a man's semen.

Do city boys have more sperm than farm boys?

This question sounds kind of kooky, but a new study contends that rural men have a lower quality sperm compared to urban dwellers. Shanna Swan, an epidemiologist and sperm researcher at the University of Missouri, Columbia, has more or less reached this conclusion. Her findings, which appear in the journal *Environmental Health Perspectives*, indicate that men in Columbia, Missouri, have inferior sperm to those men who live in Los Angeles, New York, and Minneapolis.

She studied sperm samples from 512 men whose wives were pregnant. While some of the men had substandard sperm, it wasn't so bad as to prevent them from impregnating their wives. What was most curious was the fact that the Missouri men were found to have a motile sperm count that averaged 113 million per sample. This is considered very low. Men in Minneapolis, on the other hand, average about 201 million sperm, closely followed by New Yorkers with 196 million. Los Angeles lagged behind with 162 million.

Why the low sperm count in Missouri? Swan's guess is chemicals used in farming, although she has no hard evidence to support this theory.

What does the scrotum have in common with the eyelids?

Try this one on the trivia buff at your next party. The eyelids and the scrotum are the only places on the human body that have no subcutaneous fat.

What do the soles of the feet have in common with the penis?

The soles of the feet are just as sensitive to touch as the glans of the penis, although not as enjoyable to have tickled.

What is "the celibacy of the saddle"?

Doctors have a more scientific term for it—penile anesthesia. Whatever you call it, it's the same thing—a penis that has fallen asleep. This often happens to male cyclists who have spent too much time on a bike seat. Just like a leg that gets all prickly and numb when its blood flow is reduced from sitting or lying the wrong way, the same thing can happen to a penis. Any constant pressure under the scrotum can cause this effect.

Are most men circumcised?

It depends on where you live. Circumcision is only widely practiced in the U.S., Canada, and Australia. Europe, on the other hand, isn't that big on clipping foreskins. In fact, eighty-five percent of the world's male population leave their foreskins intact.

The practice of circumcision goes all the way back to the ancient Egyptians, who believed the shedding of the foreskin would make one immortal, much in the same way the snake sheds its skin and is renewed in life. They would burn the excised foreskins as an offering to their fertility god. The Egyptians were also cleanliness freaks, and thought the foreskin unclean. (Ancient Greeks had the opposite view, and thought that circumcised men were barbarians.) From Egypt, the practice spread around the Middle East and the world.

For the Jewish people, circumcision is seen as a covenant with God. For Christians, baptism replaced this covenant. So why are so many American Christians circumcised? That's our next question.

Why are American men so widely circumcised?

Before the turn of the twentieth century, circumcision was rare in America. Its rise in popularity had nothing to do with religion or cleanliness, although this was sometimes put forth as the pretext. The Victorian-era aversion to masturbation was the real impetus for our present state of affairs. An English doctor, Sir Jonathan Hutchinson, preached that a tight-fitting foreskin sexually excited young boys and led to the scourge of self-gratification. So passionate was he that he convinced other doctors, as well as ministers and priests, that this was the case and that circumcision was the answer. Only later did the medical profession attach the issue of penile cleanliness to circumcision. Thanks a lot, Dr. Hutchinson!

Convincing doctors to perform circumcisions is one thing. But, how do you talk a mother into having her newborn go under the knife? As fate would have it, Dr. Hutchinson's crusade just happened to coincide with the period in American history when women began to go to the hospital to give birth. In 1900, less than five percent of mothers delivered in the hospital. That increased to forty percent by 1920 and to seventy-five percent by 1930. Now circumcision was an easy matter. Many a baby boy were clipped without their parents' consent. The child was simply bought back to Mom minus the foreskin. Parents tended to assume this was normal and never thought to question the practice.

Today, circumcisions are performed at various ages, depending on where you live. The Jewish faith believes in circumcising infants on the eighth day after birth. The Turks wait until the child is much older—between the ages of three and nine. These Turkish circumcisions are often group affairs, with several boys being snipped at one large ceremony. After going under the knife, the boys are presented with a diploma and must kiss the hand of the man who cut away their foreskin. A big party usually follows.

Circumcision is the most common surgery in the United States today. Some anticircumcision advocates assert that the main reason it is still so widely practiced in the United States is because of the easy profits doctors make from this outdated custom. However, the number of circumcised American men may decline, as some insurance companies begin to drop coverage for the procedure. So accustomed are we to the circumcised penis, that many women are now "acucullophiles": those who are only sexually aroused by circumcised men.

Can you be uncircumcised?

Circumcision is falling out of favor with many people. One such person is a California psychologist who wrote a book titled *The Joy of Uncircumcising*. In it, he recommends taping weights to the remaining skin and stretching it down over the head of the penis. If you persist with this bizarre technique for some years, it is said that the stretched skin will cover the glans in much the same way the original foreskin did. Good luck.

Why do some men lift weights with their penis?

There is an ancient Taoist art of body control called Chi Kung. Practitioners report that it helps fight disease and prolongs life and virility. One of the stranger manifestations of the art involves attaching weights to the base of the erect penis and doing deep knee bends and other exercises. After years of working out, some of these "athletes" can lift truly incredible amounts of weight. One

Hong Kong master—Mo Ka Wang (appropriate name)—could lift 250 pounds, two feet off of the floor.

Do men have a G-spot?

The female G-spot has been written about *ad nauseum* in countless woman's magazines. Some physiologists argue that men have their own G-spot: the prostate. It probably develops from the same kind of embryonic tissue as the female G-spot.

We hear a lot about enlarged prostates and prostate cancer but not much good news about the prostate. Well, here's some. The prostate has a great deal of erotic potential. This walnut-size gland is tucked away beneath the bladder and produces prostatic fluid, which is the main ingredient in semen. The prostate can be stimulated from without or within—by placing your fingers between the base of the scrotum and the anus and massaging, or inserting a lubricated finger into the anus and rubbing toward the stomach.

Where in the world is there a penis museum?

A man named Sigurdur Hjartarson, in Reykjavík, Iceland, could be the world's foremost "phallologist" (a guy who is obsessed with penises). He is so consumed with the penis that he opened the Icelandic Phallological Museum. Not limiting himself to the human member, Hjartarson has been collecting animal penises from all over Iceland for the past twenty-five years. He's got more than one hundred of them from every type of Icelandic animal you can think of (whales, polar bears, seals, etc.). He plans to add a human penis to his collection soon. He's already got two donors lined up.

If such esoterica interests you, for a mere $4, you can peruse the museum's collection. Last year, some 3,500 people did just that. But don't forget to check out the gift shop. It sells items like jump ropes with phallic handles and lamp shades made from dried bull and ram scrotums.

CHAPTER TWO

Victoria's Secrets

What are all those parts of a woman's genitals?

There are so many parts and names for the female genitals that many of us (i.e., most men) aren't exactly sure what is what down there. A short tour of the female anatomy will help you to better understand some of the terminology used in this chapter.

Vulva—The word "vulva" means "covering." That's pretty much what it is; all the external parts of the female genitals. It is comprised of the mons, labia, clitoris, and perineum.

Mons pubis—Also known as the mons veneris, it is the soft mound of cushiony, fatty tissue that is covered with pubic hair and sits atop the pubic bone. This area is sexually sensitive in some women and stimulation of the mons can be as exciting to some as clitoral stimulation.

Labia—These are what most people call the "lips." This is the visible part of the genitals, comprised of the outer lips (labia majora) and the inner lips (labia minora).

Labia majora—These are the two fatty folds of skin, usually with hair, that cover the labia minora, vaginal opening, and urinary opening. They contain sweat glands, oil glands, and nerve endings. When sexually excited, these outer lips swell and flatten out, due to increased blood flow, thus exposing the vaginal opening.

Labia minora—These are the inner folds of skin on either side of the vaginal opening that meet just above the clitoris, where they form a fold of skin known as the clitoral hood. They do not contain fat cells like the labia majora, but are loaded with nerve endings. These inner lips will enlarge and change in color when a woman is sexually aroused. This is called "sex skin change."

Clitoris—The clitoris is found beneath the clitoral hood. This little area of great female pleasure is discussed more in the next question.

Urethra—This opening is found just below the clitoris. It is where the urine comes out.

Vagina—Below the urethral opening is the larger vaginal opening, which is the entrance to a woman's internal genitals. The vaginal opening may be partially covered by a thin stretch of skin called the hymen.

The vagina extends about three to five inches, where it meets the cervix.

Cervix—The cervix is the lower part of the uterus. It closes off the vagina and separates it from the uterus.

Uterus—On the other side of the cervix is the uterus, or womb. It is a hollow, pear-shaped organ that is big enough to accommodate a fist and can expand enough to hold a nine-month-old fetus. The uterus is lined by the endometrium. It is designed to hold and nourish a developing fetus. It is this lining that is flushed away during menstruation.

Fallopian tubes—The uterus branches into the two fallopian tubes at its upper end. The fallopian tubes are no wider than a human hair. Each tube is about three inches long and connects the uterus to the ovaries.

Ovaries—Each pair of ovaries contains eggs and produces hormones. Every girl is born with all the eggs she will need in her lifetime. At each menstrual cycle, one of the ovaries will release one mature egg.

Like the rest of the human body, a woman's genitals come in numerous shapes, sizes, and colors. A vulva can be light pink, dark pink, peach, grayish, brown, or black. No one type is the perfect model. Some women are dissatisfied with the appearance of their genitals, thinking that they are not normal or "pretty." Each woman should accept and appreciate her genitals for the unique gift they are. Most men aren't really concerned with such matters, anyway.

How is the clitoris like an iceberg?

This has nothing to do with frigidity. It's because there's more to the clitoris than meets the eye. The clitoris is not just that little bit of tissue that you can see. Like an iceberg, only the tip of the clitoris is visible at the surface. From the Greek *klitoris*, meaning "a hill," the clitoris is a small, sensitive, erectile organ located at the upper end of the vulva. The external part that we can see is called the glans, and is similar to the male glans (head of the penis), but most of the clitoris is inside the body. Like the penis, it is composed of spongy erectile tissue, blood vessels, and nerves. Beneath the skin, the clitoris shaft divides into two legs (called the crura), like a wishbone, and extends for three inches on either side of the vaginal opening. When aroused, the whole area swells with blood and becomes firm. Since the crura run under the labia, any stimulation of the vagina, urethra, or anus indirectly stimulates the clitoris.

Where does the clitoris go during intercourse?

The female clitoris is often thought of as the female equivalent to the male penis. It has a head, called the glans, and a longer part, called the shaft. The glans is the only readily visible part of the clitoris. It looks like a shiny button. It can be found by pushing back the skin of the aforementioned clitoral hood (see previous question).

The clitoral glans has as many nerve endings as the glans of the penis; however, they are packed together much more tightly. Unlike the penis, which is used for urination, ejaculation, and also gives pleasure, the clitoris has just one function—pleasure. When a woman becomes sexually aroused, the glans and shaft both fill with blood, stiffen, and increase in size, like a penis. With increased stimulation, the clitoris becomes covered by the enlarged clitoral hood and seems to disappear. This disappearing act has a purpose. It is to protect the glans from direct stimulation, which some women can find irritating. During intercourse, the penis does not come in direct contact with the clitoris. It is the moving back and forth of the labia minora against the clitoris, caused by the thrusting penis, that produces an orgasm.

After orgasm, the blood is dispersed and the clitoris returns to normal size. If the woman does not climax, the clitoris may remain engorged with blood for a few hours, which some women find uncomfortable—the female equivalent of "blue balls." (See related question on page 9.)

What is the most sensitive area of the vagina?

The vagina is the internal portion of a woman's sex organ. It starts at the vaginal opening and extends up about three to five inches where it meets the cervix.

There are three layers of tissue that line the vagina. The outermost layer (the one you can touch) is a lining of folded mucous membranes, similar to those inside of the mouth. The middle layer is comprised of muscles and the innermost layer is fibrous tissue.

Most of the time, the vagina is like a collapsed tube. It doesn't open up into a true tube unless something it inserted into it. The muscle layer allows the vagina to fit snugly around objects of varying sizes. Whether it be a baby passing through, a large or small penis, or a finger, the muscle layer will expand and contract as needed. The walls of the vagina are not rich in nerve endings. Ninety percent of the vaginal nerves are found in the lower third, near the vaginal opening. This is why a woman derives more pleasure from having the lower vagina stimulated than the upper two-thirds.

How does the vagina lubricate itself?

The vagina does not contain any secretory glans, per se. So how does it produce lubrication? When a woman is sexually excited, the blood swelling the veins in the vagina pushes against the vaginal tissues and forces out droplets of tissue fluids, which act as a sexual lubricant. Without this fluid or some artificial lubricant, intercourse would be painful for most women. As a woman ages, she produces less lubrication, especially after menopause.

Do women have wet dreams?

While normally associated with younger men, some women do indeed have wet dreams in their sleep. Wet dreams are most common for women in their 40s, although, according to a Kinsey study, less than forty percent report having them. The female wet dream does not involve ejaculation, per se, but an increase in vaginal lubrication. As with male erections, these lubrications happen about four to six times a night, and help to clean out the cervix, as does masturbation.

What is the ballooning effect?

We all know that a man's penis enlarges when he is aroused. Likewise, a woman's vagina increases in size when she is sexually aroused, as during foreplay. When stimulated, the inner two-thirds of the vagina widen and extend about two inches in length. Masters and Johnson dubbed this phenomenon "ballooning." This protects a woman from the thrusting of a large penis. At the same time that the inner two-thirds are ballooning, the outer third is narrowing and swelling up, getting tighter.

This vasoconstriction is a result of blood engorging the tissues. The tighter vaginal opening helps to grip the penis and gives the man greater stimulation. Thus, it may be worth a man's while to engage in a little foreplay in order to enhance his lovemaking pleasure. The first one-third of the vagina has the most nerve endings and stimulation of this area also gives the woman the greatest arousal. In other words, while penis length is thought to be of utmost importance, it's the girth that really gets the ladies going.

Can a woman have her vagina tightened?

If your man's penis isn't big enough, you can take matters into your own hands and have your vagina tightened up. The process, called "female genitalia enhancement," is accomplished by removing fat from the thighs, which is then emulsified and injected into the outer labia. The labia are then squeezed to reposition the fat up into the vaginal walls. After a successful operation, you will feel much tighter to your partner and he will feel much bigger to you. This procedure eliminates the need for him to be enhanced in size.

Who discovered the G-spot?

You would think it would have been a woman, right? After all, they have them. Well, the first person to propose the existence of the mythical G-spot was one Dr. Ernst Gräfenberg, in 1950, in the *International Journal of Sexology*. It is a bean-shaped area of erectile tissue just behind the front wall of the vagina, between the back of the pubic bone and the cervix. No one seemed to notice the good doctor's discovery for over three decades. It didn't even have a name until two scientists—John D. Perry and Beverly Whipple—called it the "G-spot," in honor of Gräfenberg (hence the capital "G"). In 1982, along with Alice Kahn Ladas, they dropped the "G" bomb on the public with the publication of *The G-spot and Other Recent Discoveries About Sexuality*.

If you can find the G-spot, do a little experimenting. It is said that G-spot orgasms are different from clitoral ones. While a clitoral orgasm is pretty much a genital area affair, the G-spot orgasm is felt more throughout the whole body.

The G-spot also has some pain-blocking properties. Pressure on this spot can double a female's pain threshold. This is useful during childbirth, when the baby comes out and presses on the G-spot, reducing mom's pain.

Do women ejaculate?

We tend to think of the male orgasm when we hear the word "ejaculate." But remarkably, some women do, at times, ejaculate fluid from the urethra when they have an orgasm. It is usually associated with direct stimulation of the G-spot, but can also occur during cunnilingus or manual stimulation.

One reason many women do not ejaculate is that the urge to ejaculate feels similar to the urge to urinate, so they hold it back. When it does occur, fluid is discharged in amounts ranging from a few drops to several teaspoons. Analysis shows that the fluid is more like the fluid produced in the male prostate than like urine. While some women may lose control of their bladder during orgasm, it is more likely that the sensation they are feeling is that of ejaculation.

Even today, this process is not fully understood. It is believed that the ejaculate is fluid released from the Skene's glands. These specialized tissues surround the urethra. They are somewhat akin to the prostate. Apparently some women produce more of this fluid than others, which accounts for the fact that only a few women notice ejaculation. Even women who do ejaculate may only do so sporadically.

Do all women have a hymen?

The hymen, or "maidenhead," is a little flap of tissue that partially covers the vaginal opening at birth. It is named after the Greek god of marriage and has no known biological function. Some consider it nature's little tamper-proof safety seal. Many cultures rely on the blood and pain produced by the bride's broken hymen on her wedding night to verify that she is a virgin. However, not all hymens necessarily produce blood when ruptured during the first full penetration (intercourse). Some women never even have a hymen, or have one that stretches but does not break. Other hymens may break from activities totally unrelated to sex, such as strenuous exercising or insertion of a tampon, or for no reason at all. Occasionally, a woman must have her hymen surgically removed before childbirth, as it is so small or flexible that it remained intact during intercourse.

Can a woman fake virginity?

There is really no good medical reason for modern women to have hymens. Nevertheless, for centuries, women have gone to extremes to preserve their hymens, or at least the appearance of an intact hymen.

Since early times, women have had to pass the test of virginity. The Romans would lower a bride onto a phallic-shaped stone sculpture representing one of their gods of fertility—Mutunus Tutunus. A millennium later, Buddhist monks in Cambodia routinely deflowered girls before their weddings. Even today, the deflowering of girls by priests is still practiced in parts of India.

Clever maidens devised several techniques to restore the appearance of virginity. Sponges soaked in blood could be inserted in the vagina, as could small fish bladders filled with blood. Since not all virgins bleed, methods of restoring the tightness of the vagina were also employed. Strong astringents, such as vinegar, myrrh water, and infusions of acorns and sloes were commonly used.

During the 1920s, 1930s, and 1940s, a minor surgical procedure was performed by doctors in the United States on young females about to be wed. Known as a "lover's knot," the operation involved joining the inner vaginal lips with stitches. When the marriage was consummated, the stitches would rip, causing bleeding and pain, simulating the breaking of the hymen, and thus preserving the lady's honor. To this day, some 30,000 to 40,000 similar operations are performed each year in Tokyo, where virginity is still revered.

Who were the first women to increase the size of their bosoms?

If you think about it, the idea of surgically implanting bags of gel into a woman's breasts seems a bit drastic. American women were not the first to try to enlarge the size of their breasts from within. That distinction belongs to the Japanese.

The prostitutes of post–World War II Japan catered to the large American occupation force. They found that the GIs were used to the larger American breasts of the women back home. The relatively diminutive bosom of the Japanese was less of a turn-on for them, and the gals with bigger boobs did a better business. To remedy this situation, the Japanese prostitutes resorted to getting injections of saline solution or goat's milk to swell the breasts. Both were quickly absorbed into the body and caused infections. Paraffin wax was tried. Although it stayed in the bosom longer, the procedure was painful and the results were lumpy. Doctors then came upon the idea of injecting the women with liquid silicone, a brand-new product from Dow Corning, which was inert but hard to find.

Silicone had several military applications and was not readily available, except on the black market. It was an immediate hit. The breasts could be greatly increased in size with a soft, natural feel. Silicone was not absorbed into the body so the look lasted and complications were few. It didn't take long for news of this new wonder chemical's magical breast-enhancement potential to travel back to American plastic surgeons.

Who invented breast implants?

By the 1950s, women were placing little bags of silicone in their bras to give the illusion of full breasts. It wasn't until 1962 that Houston plastic surgeons Thomas Cronin and Frank Gerow decided to stick silicone bags directly into the breasts. (David Schwimmer starred in a somewhat silly 1997 docudrama about these guys, called *Breast Men*, that occasionally runs on cable.)

Dow began manufacturing gel bags for this express purpose. By the early 1970s, tens of thousands of women received implants, and many surgeons became wealthy as a result. But all was not rosy. Some women began to complain that their implants leaked. In 1977, a jury awarded a woman $170,000 for her leaky implants, so Dow brought out water-based bags in 1978. More bad news was to follow. Many claimed that leaky silicone implants were causing health problems. In 1984, a woman won a court decision charging that implants cause autoimmune disease. The lawsuits continued, and by 1992, the FDA banned the use of silicone implants. A $4.25 billion settlement offer was made by Dow and others in 1994, and in May of 1995, Dow Corning filed for bankruptcy.

Interestingly, to this day, it has never been scientifically proven that the leaky implants caused the health problems that brought about the downfall of Dow Corning.

How many women get breast implants?

There were 200,000 breast-implant procedures performed in 2002. Two thousand of those operations were performed on girls under the age of eighteen. Over ninety-seven percent of breast augmentation surgeries are performed on white women. The number of breast augmentation procedures rose 500 percent in the last decade, with a ninety percent increase between 1997 and 1999.

The woman with the biggest fake boobs is French porn star Lolo Ferrari. She has undergone at least twenty-two augmentation operations to achieve her seventy-three-inch bustline.

One side note: Ferrari died in March 2000 from an apparent overdose of prescription drugs. However, her husband/manager, Eric Vigne, was arrested on suspicion of murder by French police in 2002, after it was subsequently determined that she died of suffocation.

Do breast implants guarantee you more cleavage?

The creation of cleavage is one big reason that women want implants. However, increasing the size of your breasts doesn't necessarily give you more cleavage. Big breasts and cleavage are not the same thing. Cleavage is the depression formed between a woman's breasts. It is dependent upon the breasts being fairly close together. Women whose breasts are naturally wide apart will generally not get more cleavage from breast augmentation.

What are some other breast-enhancement methods?

There are several, but they are all pretty much bogus. Women have tried exercises, creams, suction devices, herbal pills, and even hypnotherapy. Some hypnotherapists convince unwitting women that by thinking about having big breasts, under hypnosis, they can increase their size. The theory goes that by having the patient convince her hypothalamus to trigger the pituitary gland to release breast-enlarging hormones, her bosom can blossom. Seems like a stretch. If it were this simple, millions of women would not be going under the knife.

Are breast implants tax deductible?

They may be if you are a stripper. The United States Tax Court has ruled that, in some cases, breast implants may be deductible as a business expense for go-go dancers.

In 1988, exotic dancer Cynthia S. Hess, known professionally as "Chesty Love," was allowed a $2,088 deduction for depreciation on her surgically implanted breasts. Judge Joan Seitz Pate, noting that her two artificially enhanced fifty-six FF breasts, each weighing ten pounds, would be uncomfortable and burdensome, ruled that the only sane reason to buy such big ones would be to make money.

Her enormous breasts also proved to be a hazard to her health. In December of that same year, Hess slipped on some ice and ruptured one of them. Talk about quick depreciation!

Do men really prefer large breasts?

Maybe women are more hung up with large breasts than men. At least that's the finding of one recent survey conducted by MyVoice.co.uk for National Cleavage Day, on March 30, 2002. Of the 1,222 male respondents, eighty-one percent said they would want medium-sized breasts if they were women. The survey also found that while most men like to *fantasize* about women with large breasts, fifty-three percent said they actually *prefer* medium-sized breasts, fourteen percent said they prefer large ones, five percent prefer small, and twenty-eight percent aren't fussy about size at all.

So ladies, no matter what size your breasts, there are men out there who like you just the way you are.

Do men get breast implants?

Amazingly, the answer is yes. According to the United States Center for Health Statistics, two percent of the silicone breast-augmentation operations performed have been done on men. Some ten thousand men a year received the implants before the silicone controversy arose.

How many women have breast reductions?

While millions of women are obsessed with getting big, fake-looking boobs, some want to go the other way. Many women find that their breasts are just too darn big. They may feel their large bosom is unsightly or cumbersome. Also, some breast implant recipients wish to go back to their natural state. Up to 80,000 breast-reduction procedures are performed every year. Brazil, a country more interested in a woman's derriere than her bustline, is the world leader in per capita breast reductions.

Why do a woman's nipples get hard?

Men and women both have nipples. Obviously, female breasts receive rather more attention than do their male counterparts. We'll confine our discussion to women's breasts.

The female breast contains about fifteen to twenty milk-producing sacs, called milk glands. Milk ducts lead from these glands to the nipples. That's the functional part of the breast. The rest is the fatty tissue that men find so interesting. The nipple, which also interests men to no end, is the pencil-eraser-shaped tissue that protrudes from the center of the breast (as if you needed to be told that). It contains many nerve endings and thin muscle fibers. These nerve endings make the nipple sensitive to touch and the muscle fibers enable it to become erect.

Unlike penises, nipples become erect from muscle contractions, not blood engorgement. About ten percent of women have inverted nipples that stick in instead of out. This condition is normal and has no effect on one's ability to nurse a child.

Are all women aroused by having their breasts caressed?

During sex, a woman's nipples and areolae may swell and the nipples may become erect. The veins in the breast may also become more visible, as the blood flow through them increases. The areolae will return to normal shortly after orgasm, but the nipple erections may last for hours, especially in older women.

However, not all women find the stimulation of the nipples and breasts all that pleasurable. Some women don't even experience nipple erections during sex. Despite what you may see in the porn movies, many women don't get off on having their breasts caressed or sucked on. There are others, however, who get very excited from breast stimulation. In fact, one in one hundred women can achieve orgasm through breast stimulation alone. Some nursing mothers can even experience orgasms.

Why the differing reactions to breast stimulation?

One theory holds that a woman's response to having her breasts stimulated in a sexual way has something to do with her own personal relationship with them. If she likes the way they look and is comfortable with them, she will enjoy having them fondled and caressed. If she doesn't like her breasts or finds them unattractive, she will be less receptive to having them stimulated. Go figure.

What are the little bumps on a woman's areolae?

The round, pigmented tissue that surrounds the nipple is the areola. This area also contains nerve endings and muscle fibers that assist the nipple in becoming erect. The bumps that one often sees on the areola are oil glands, known as Montgomery's glands, which secrete a lubricant to protect the nipple and make breast-feeding easier.

Female nipples and areolae can vary widely in size and color. During pregnancy, a woman's nipples darken considerably, and remain so for some time.

How many women have an extra nipple?

Men love a woman's nipples, usually in pairs. But many women, one in every two hundred in fact, have a third nipple. Extra, or "supernumerary" nipples, are generally small, and most resemble a mole or freckle. However, they can also be the same size as a normal nipple. They may be found on or below the breasts, and some can even lactate during pregnancy. The condition is considered normal, but it is possible to have them removed by a plastic surgeon if desired.

Rumor has it that not only did Ann Boleyn, second wife of Henry VIII, have six fingers on each hand, but she also possessed a third breast. Even this sexual "enhancement" didn't save her from the tower.

What's the most breasts a woman ever had?

There have been reports that in extremely rare cases, some women have had up to ten functional breasts. The condition is known as "polymastia." In men, there is a similar condition called "gynecomastia," where the poor fellow develops multiple enlarged pectorals.

Is regular sex good for you?

There is proof that intimate sexual contact with a man is good for a woman's health. A study was conducted by the University of Pennsylvania Medical School and the Monell Chemical Senses Center involving nearly celibate women and male sweat. One group of sexually inactive females had the essence of male sweat rubbed under their noses three times a week for three months. A second control group was rubbed with alcohol. The sweat-smelling women were found to have developed regular menstrual cycles of 29.5 days, as opposed a range of about 26 to 33 days before the study. The control group showed no such change.

Researchers concluded that some kind of pheromone in male sweat, such as is found in the armpits, genital area, and around the nipples, may have had an effect on the women's vomeronasal organ, located in the nose. This may have not only promoted a regular menstrual cycle, but also may have increased fertility and caused a milder menopause. The best way for a woman to smell these sweat pheromones would be through sexual contact. This beats rubbing a man's sweat under your nose, and is a lot more fun.

Is intercourse beneficial to a woman during her period?

Some people enjoy sexual intercourse during a woman's period, many don't. There is absolutely nothing wrong with the practice, and it may actually be good for a woman. The muscle contractions that occur during an orgasm can help to push excess fluids out of the uterus and thus reduce cramping. A woman also produces more vaginal lubricants when she is menstruating, making intercourse more pleasurable to the man. So, go ahead. Just remember that it *is* possible to get pregnant during this time.

When does a girl become fertile?

The immediate answer would be when she goes through puberty and starts to mensturate. In fact, that usually is not the case. The average age of first menstruation is twelve and a half. While a girl's first menstruation is a key signal of becoming a fertile woman, it is not the milestone many believe it to be. Many hormonal changes have to occur in a girl's body to enable her to conceive. These changes may not be complete for some time after puberty. This is known as the "adolescence sterility period." Even more changes need to occur to be able to carry a fetus to full term. In some girls, these conditions may not be present for up to two years after she starts menstruating. But don't take this to mean that a girl, at any age, should have unprotected sex.

What is female circumcision?

You may never have heard of it, but female circumcision is a ghastly practice that has already been performed on some 135 million women in the Middle East and Africa and continues at a rate of about two million a year. This form of mutilation involves the removal of all or part of the labia and clitoris, without anesthetic, and usually under less than sterile conditions. Many deaths have resulted.

There are twenty-eight African countries currently practicing female circumcision. In Somalia, ninety-eight percent of the women are mutilated in this fashion. Female circumcision is generally done in fundamentalist Muslim societies, where they believe it to be the best way to ensure marital fidelity. The procedure reduces a woman's sexual pleasure, thus reducing her desire to cheat on her husband. There is some hope. Several nations, including Egypt, have recently outlawed this abomination.

In the past, clitoridectomies were performed on harem girls. A village woman would pinch the clitoris between the thumb and forefinger and slice it off with a razor. The practice was said to enhance vaginal orgasms and discourage any lesbianism that might occur in the harem. A more bizarre form of clitoridectomy was performed on the girls of the Nandi tribe in Africa. Stinging nettles would be rubbed on the clitoris, causing it to become inflamed. It was then burned out with hot coals. Even some American women went under the knife as recently as the early 1900s, to prevent masturbation.

What is so important about a woman's waist to hip ratio?

There seems to be a universal consensus about the ideal female waist to hip ratio. While in men, a small difference between waist and hip size results in an ideal ratio of 0.9, females tend to have a greater difference between waist and hip size, something closer to a ratio of 0.7.

In childhood and old age, a female's waist and hips are somewhat closer in their measurements. It is during the most fertile years—the late teens and early twenties—that a woman generally has those curvaceous hips and flat stomachs that men find so alluring. This is a plus for attracting a mate, but it is also a plus when it comes time to conceive. A study of fertility clinic records shows that women with the 0.7 ratio (those with a classic hourglass figure) are thirty percent more likely to conceive than are those with a more masculine ratio of 0.8.

CHAPTER THREE

Getting it Up!

What is impotence?

We don't really call it impotence anymore. The politically correct term is "erectile dysfunction" (ED). Whatever you want to call it, ED is defined as the inability to produce an erection capable of vaginal penetration, although it's not really that simple. Many men can't just summon up an erection out of the blue. Failure to get it up once in a while when depressed, stressed out, tired, drug or alcohol impaired, or not properly stimulated, is okay, and is not ED. Lack of sexual desire isn't impotence either. Impotence is not being able to get it up when you *want* to. Lack of libido is another story.

There are many possible reasons for ED. Twenty percent of the time it is a result of psychological problems; the rest of the time there are physical problems. As men get older their chance of ED goes up. At the age of forty, about five percent have it. By age sixty-five, some twenty-five percent of men are impotent. Other physical reasons for ED are low testosterone, diseases or injury, and side effects from medications. To determine if you have physical impotence, consult a doctor.

What causes impotence?

Feelings of stress and anxiety can make you temporarily impotent, but won't curb your desire. On the other hand, feelings of depression and anger can cause you to lose desire but still be able to get an erection. One way to tell if your impotence is physical or mental is to take note of whether you get erections in your sleep. If your impotence is just psychological, you should still have nighttime erections. If you suspect physical impotence, see a urologist, who will test your veins and arterial blood flow. By injecting you with an erection-inducing drug, he can tell right away if your problem is physical. Most of these problems are treatable with surgery.

Who invented Viagra?

The testosterone levels of men begins to drop by one percent a year after reaching age forty. With this reduction in testosterone comes a reduction in libido and the angle of erection. For some, it means impotence. Who knew there was a wonder drug out there waiting to be discovered? Surely not the people at Pfizer. As with many of humankind's greatest discoveries, this one was purely accidental.

In 1989, Pfizer was developing a drug to treat angina. They noticed that the patients receiving the new drug seemed to take a great interest in any passing female nurse. They put two and two together and came up with one billion. That's the dollar amount Viagra currently generates every year!

In their testing of Viagra, Pfizer used a device called a Rigiscan to measure the erection responses of thousands of men. Eighty percent had improved erections. It was found that Viagra caused increased blood flow to the penis. It is not a hormone or an aphrodisiac.

Viagra was made available in 1998. Bob Dole was one of the first pitchmen. He appealed to older men. Mark Martin, the race car driver, pitched to a younger, physically fit crowd. But Viagra hardly needed pitchmen to promote it. The drug was the most successful prescription in history. In one week alone, 120,000 prescriptions were written. Millions started using it, even at $10 a pill. So far, thirty million Americans have taken advantage of the drug. Millions more probably could benefit from Viagra. So Pfizer is working on a gel form that can be applied directly to the penis and will act in fifteen minutes.

Other new impotence drugs on the horizon are Melanotan, which will give you an erection and a tan (not a bad deal); apomorphine, a drug also used to treat Parkinson's disease; Levitra, and Cialis.

How does Viagra help preserve endangered wildlife?

Talk about a miracle drug. Not only does Viagra free millions of men from the curse of impotence, it is now claimed by some that it also helps save the lives of countless endangered species.

As you may know, many rare animals are killed each year to obtain various parts of their anatomy that some people believe are aphrodisiacs. The introduction of the drug Viagra has lessened the demand for many of these animal extracts, at least in the United States and Canada.

Researchers in Australia and Canada have shown that since the introduction of Viagra in 1998, the trading in some animal parts has dropped by up to seventy percent. Studies were done on three select, legally traded species—hooded seals and harp seals, which are hunted for their genitalia, and Alaskan reindeer, which are hunted for their antler velvet. The price of harp seal penises declined from $110 per organ to $15 by 1999. The number of seal penises traded went from 40,000 per year to 20,000. The market for antler velvet fell by seventy-two percent, from $700,000 in 1997 to $200,000 in 1998.

Viagra tends to be cheaper and more effective than traditional medicines. However, many cultures around the world don't have easy access to Viagra and still tend to prefer their more familiar animal-based remedies.

What drugs can produce erections?

Yes, we're talking about legal drugs, of course. Some men can benefit from injecting drugs such as papaverine or phentolamine, or a combination of the two, directly into the base of the penis shaft. These drugs relax the penile muscles, allowing blood to enter the penis, thus making it erect. This is called a "pharmacologic erection," and is useful for men with "neurologic impotence," whose penile tissue and blood supply are normal, but whose penile nerve response is abnormal.

Other drugs can be inserted into the urethra (the hole at the tip of the penis). One such drug called alprostadil is a suppository pellet that a man can insert directly into the urethra by using a plastic applicator. He must massage himself for a few minutes to help dissolve and disperse the drug. The drug relaxes the muscles in the penis, allowing blood to flow in. Within ten to fifteen minutes, he should have an erection that will last thirty to sixty minutes.

A topical nitroglycerine cream is also available that can be directly applied to the penis. It dilates the blood vessels in the penis, producing an erection.

Is any impotence drug better than Viagra?

Viagra is the wonder drug that has re-energized the sex lives of countless men around the world. One dose of Viagra lasts for eight to twelve hours. Pretty good, right? Well, a new impotence drug is coming down the pike. It's called Cialis and it's being developed by Eli Lilly and Company and the Icos Corporation. It works in a manner similar to Viagra, which targets the enzyme that increases blood flow to the penis.

While twelve hours of mojo is great for men with erectile dysfunction, thirty-six hours would be fantastic. The two companies claim that Cialis can enable a majority of men to have two successful sexual sessions thirty-six hours after ingesting the drug. Side effects include headaches and upset stomachs. This is a significant breakthrough because many men find the relatively small window of time during which Viagra is effective can cramp their style.

Will there ever be a female Viagra?

Okay, so science has solved the sexual dysfunction of millions of men with Viagra. What about the dysfunctional ladies out there? A 1999 study found that forty-three percent of women suffer from some kind of female sexual dysfunction (FSD). For men, there is basically one sexual dysfunction—impotence. Women, on the other hand, have four types of dysfunction: insufficient lubrication, lack of desire, pain during intercourse, and trouble reaching orgasm. It's tough to come up with one pill that will solve four different problems. Viagra can help the twenty percent of the FSD population with lubrication problems.

Those women that have a lack of sexual desire can be helped by adjusting their estrogen/testosterone ratios. Testosterone is very important to a woman's libido. Her sex drive is triggered by tiny secretions of testosterone in the ovaries and adrenal glands. These secretions decrease with the onset of old age. Procter & Gamble has come out with testosterone patches that may help.

An over-the-counter sex enhancer for women has just come on the market worldwide. Called Finally . . . The Solution For Women, it is a topical cream made from natural ingredients, pH balanced and hormone free. Its makers claim that it is effective in heightening and prolonging sexual pleasure by increasing a woman's sensitivity and stimulation. It is supposed to begin working in five to seven minutes and last up to forty-five minutes. Does the stuff really work? Well, for $5.99 you can buy some and make up your own mind.

What devices can produce an artificial erection?

The "lengths" some men will go to for an erection are mindboggling. Several contraptions exist to give men an erection, for the times when no other method will suffice.

Vacuum Pump—This type of device has an acrylic cylinder that fits over the flaccid penis. It is connected to a hand or battery-operated pump that creates a vacuum and draws blood into the penis. Upon swelling, a ring is fastened around the base of the erect penis. This maintains the erection by preventing the blood from flowing back out.

Flexible Implants—Another type of device consists of two flexible cylinders that are implanted into the shaft of the penis. The rods have an outer silicone coating, covering a stainless steel core or interlocking plastic joints. Following implantation, the penis is semirigid and can be bent up for sex or down for storage when not in use. There is no increase in size, however.

Inflatable Implants—A second kind of implant, known as an "internal penile pump," involves two inflatable cylinders in the shaft of the penis attached to a fluid reservoir, and a pump housed in the lower abdomen and the scrotum. The pump can be squeezed several times to force the fluid into the shaft cylinders, causing an erection. Upon completion of its duty, the erection can be deflated by pushing a release valve that allows the fluid to return back to the reservoir.

At a cost of $10,000 to $15,000, these devices are usually a last resort for desperate men. Happily, many insurance plans and Medicare cover penile implants. About ninety percent of implants used today are the pump type, and ten percent are malleable rods. Since the 1970s, over 300,000 men have received inflatable penile implants. About 20,000 men a year choose to treat their impotence with implants.

What does the future hold for impotent men?

Within about fifteen years, the field of gene therapy may replace drug therapy to help treat impotence. By introducing genes into the body via a virus carrier, normal sexual functions may be restored. Until then, the pharmaceutical companies can count on raking in the profits.

However, if you are into electrical devices, a Norwegian inventor is testing a battery-operated penis ring that he claims can take the place of Viagra or penile injections. Electrical engineer Birger

Orten's invention is a thin ring with "advanced energy trans-feral," whatever that means. It is fitted around the base of the penis and has immediate stimulatory results. There are said to be no side effects. Preliminary human tests have been encouraging. After further testing, the ring will be offered for sale.

What is the most expensive aphrodisiac?

The herb ginseng is revered as an aphrodisiac in the Orient. Roots that resemble the human anatomy in any way are the most valuable—selling for between $100 and $500 a pound. The age of the root is also very important. The older the better. The record price paid for a root of perfect shape and age was $180,000!

Another expensive aphrodisiac fancied in the Far East are North American bear gall bladders. They fetch between $400 and $600. Seahorses and deer antlers are also quite popular.

What aphrodisiac used to be picked with a dog's tail?

In days gone by, a plant could develop a supernatural reputa-tion if its attributes were sufficiently bizarre. One such plant is the mandrake, or *Mandragora officinarum*, which is a small perennial herb found in the Mediterranean region. Related to the deadly nightshade, it is a toxic plant. The roots are said to resemble a little man, including penis. (This resemblance to a little human is used to great cinematic effect in the movie *Harry Potter and the Chamber of Secrets*, except the penis part!) Adding to its "magical" qualities is the fact that the berries can phosphoresce, or emit light. The ancients believed that the mandrake, worn as a amulet, was a charm against demons and a promoter of love and fertility.

Mandrake is one of the first plants mentioned in the Bible. In Genesis 30:14–16, Rachel agrees to let her husband Jacob sleep with Leah in exchange for her mandrakes.

One problem with the mandrake, however, was harvesting it. While its glow made it easy to find, they believed that merely touching it could prove fatal. The best way to get it out of the ground was to dig all around it, until just a little bit of the roots remained in the soil. Then one end of a rope was tied around the plant and the other end tied around a dog's tail. When the dog was called, he pulled out the plant, roots and all. Mandrake's fertility powers were written about up into the seventeenth century.

Do NOT ingest mandrake in any way! It is a poisonous plant. There is also an American mandrake plant, *Polypodium peltatum*, which is sold by herb companies under the name "mandrake roots." It is a totally different plant.

What is the only herbal aphrodisiac approved by the FDA?

Yohimbe comes from the bark of a tropical West African tree and is the source of the pharmaceutical drug yohimbine. The Bantu people traditionally used yohimbe as a sacrament in matrimony orgy rituals that were known to last up to fifteen days, with doses increasing as the ceremonies wore on. In high doses, yohimbe is also a hallucinogen.

Known as the "herbal Viagra," yohimbe is the only herb listed in the *Physicians Desk Reference* as promoting sexual function. Yohimbe's power comes from a combination of plant alkaloids. The alkaloid yohimbine blocks alpha-2-adrenergic nerve activity, which normally would constrict the blood vessels. As such, the vessels are allowed to dilate, thus facilitating increased blood flow. Increased blood flow equals better erections.

What is "horny goat weed"?

Horny goat weed (*Epimedium*), as you probably guessed, is an herbal sex stimulant. This aphrodisiac is said to promote blood flow to the genitals and improve sexual energy. It originates in China, where it is called yin-yang, because it increases sexual pleasure for the female (yin) as well as the male (yang). Horny goat weed lowers the blood pressure by dilating capillaries and blood vessels. It also lowers adrenal production, which slows the blood flow to the genitals. The plant contains testosterone-like alkaloids and sterols as well. It is available online.

What is "Spanish fly"?

"Spanish fly" is an aphrodisiac that has been around for a couple thousand years. It is made from the dried wings of South American meloid beetles. Spanish fly contains a chemical called cantharidin, that, aside from making you nauseous, makes your urinary tract itch and produces a long-lasting, painful erection. Apparently, the best way to scratch this itch is to ejaculate. One had to be careful with the dosage, as too much can cause kidney damage, convulsions, or death. No wonder it fell out of favor in the nineteenth century.

Is there a new female aphrodisiac on the horizon?

Yes, and it's called PT-141. Not a very catchy name, but tests have shown it will drive a normal, healthy woman to a state of high sexual arousal. The drug is a nasal spray that is being tested by Palatin Technologies in New Jersey.

What is different about PT-141, as opposed to a drug like Viagra, is that it directly targets the brain's sexual arousal center. Viagra, on the other hand, acts by directly stimulating the blood flow to the genitals. This is why it could be very helpful to the many women who suffer from a lack of libido, not physiological problems.

The company hopes to market the drug in two or three years. Their target audience would be women with sexual problems. They don't foresee its misuse by men to seduce unsuspecting women, as it is a nasal spray. Even if one could trick a woman into taking it, PT-141 wouldn't make a woman interested in a guy that she previously would have been uninterested in.

What is air-conditioned underwear?

As you may know, one of the more common reasons for male infertility is a low sperm count. You may also know that wearing tight-fitting underwear can contribute to a lower sperm count. (A man is considered infertile if his count is lower than sixty million, of which only forty percent are motile.) But did you know that German doctors have come up with air-conditioned underpants? Doctors at the University of Frankfurt set out to prove men are more fertile when their testicles are kept cool. One of the reasons that the testicles hang outside of the body cavity is to keep them four degrees cooler than the normal body temperature of 98.6°F. What the scientists came up with is a battery-powered fan that clips on a belt. The fan blows air into tubes that run down to the groin, where nozzles direct air flow. Straps attached to the belt wrap around the thighs, holding the tubes and nozzles in place.

The doctors say the contraption works, lowering the testicular temperature to at least one degree Centigrade below normal. A study was conducted on twenty men who wore the device every night for twelve weeks. Preliminary results showed that not only did sperm production increase, but the little guys were much more active.

Those of you who don't fancy such a cumbersome remedy can try wearing boxers during the day and nothing at night.

Who performed the first human artificial insemination?

The first recorded case of a successful human artificial insemination was that inspired by Scottish surgeon John Hunter in 1785. The good doctor advised a couple to warm a syringe, collect the man's semen in it, and immediately squirt it into her vagina. This is said to have resulted in conception. Other cases of human artificial insemination may have preceded Dr. Hunter's, but none have been authenticated. In 1785, M. Thouret of the University of Paris medical faculty is said to have squirted a sample of his own semen into his wife's vagina using a tin syringe. It is known that Arabs were probably using artificial insemination on horses as early as the fourteenth century.

The first artificial insemination using donated sperm is said to have taken place in 1884, in Philadelphia. However, there was some trickery involved. The anesthetized woman was unaware that her sterile husband had instructed the doctor to use another man's semen.

By the mid-1950s, frozen sperm was being used successfully to impregnate women. It was not until 1964 that the first sperm repositories (banks) opened in Tokyo and Iowa City. Today's sperm banks keep sperm frozen at −321 degrees Fahrenheit. Screened donors get about $50 per specimen and can make up to $5,000 per year.

Where can you go to have your male sperm separated from your female sperm?

Despite the concerns of many people who think this technology will allow us to play God, you can now have your sperm separated to help you father a boy or a girl. MircoSort, of Fairfax, Virginia, has developed a sperm sorter for just such a purpose.

Normally, you have a fifty-fifty chance of having a boy or girl, as both sperm types are produced in equal number. MicroSort uses a flow cytometer to separate X (female) and Y (male) chromosome-bearing sperm cells. The X chromosome is substantially larger than the Y chromosome, and thus contains more DNA. The amount of DNA in a sperm cell can be measured and then directed into two distinct streams by the flow cytometer.

The procedure can greatly increase your odds of determining your child's sex. For female sperm selection, the process is eighty-eight percent effective; for male sperm, it is seventy-three percent accurate. The mother can use intrauterine insemination or in vitro fertilization. Either way, you will have to go to Fairfax to have the sperm separated.

This seems to make a lot more sense than some practices of the past. A pregnant woman in ancient Greece would eat the testicle of a rooster if she wanted a boy. During the nineteenth century, it was thought by some that if the man climaxed first, the resultant child would be a girl. If that were the case, there would be a lot more girls running around than boys!

Where can a lesbian couple go to get sperm?

Obviously, many lesbians wishing to become pregnant don't really want a man to inseminate them. But where to get the sperm? No need to worry; you can now all but eliminate a man from your sperm acquisition needs by logging on to mannotincluded.com. Just fill out an online registration form, pay your registration fee, and you will be given a password to access their main database and search out a donor that is right for you. (Yes, it is a man. They're not totally out of the picture yet!)

Once you have picked out three possible donors, you get to talk with a female counselor to help you make your final decision. Next, figure out when you are going to be fertile and the freshly donated sperm will be shipped to you for easy at-home insemination, or you can go to their clinic. What could be easier?

Can giving head make your pregnancy safer and more successful?

Researchers at the University of Adelaide in Australia have found some evidence that a woman who performs fellatio on a man has a better chance of later becoming impregnated by his sperm. Their study found that semen contains a growth factor that encourages a woman's immune system to accept sperm. Regular exposure to a man's sperm, especially by mouth, helps her immune system to recognize her partner's sperm as safe.

Some problems that can occur during pregnancy are associated with the mother's immune system "battling" with the fetus as a foreign body. Many of the fetal "foreign" proteins come from the father's genes, so getting regular exposure to them before pregnancy helps mom's body to recognize and accept them.

Professor Gustaaf Dekker compared forty-one women with pre-eclampsia, a condition of high blood pressure during pregnancy, and forty-four without the condition. He found a much higher percentage of the women without the condition practiced fellatio. Swallowing makes the protective effect even more pronounced. The good professor recommends women having trouble carrying a pregnancy to full term to practice oral sex and to swallow.

How much does the frequency of intercourse per month increase the odds of getting pregnant?

So you're trying to have a baby. You might think that having sex every day would dramatically increase your odds of conception. It will, but probably not as much as you may have thought. If a fertile woman has intercourse once a week during her menstrual cycle, she has a fifteen percent chance of getting pregnant. If she has sex every other day, the odds more than double to thirty-three percent. However, having intercourse every day only slightly increases the chance of conception to thirty-seven percent. So you may as well pace yourself.

CHAPTER FOUR

Sponges, Caps, and Pills

What were the first forms of contraception?

The earliest forms of birth control are believed to have been herbs used during the late Paleolithic period. At that time, the male's role in reproduction was unknown. Although they didn't realize that intercourse was connected with pregnancy, early humans curiously enough figured out that women could do certain things to prevent or curtail it. The early herbal contraceptives were probably similar to the ones that Native Americans more recently brewed into herbal teas. The Hopis, for instance, used dried jack-in-the-pulpit. Modern science has found that some of these herbal contraceptives are somewhat effective.

Humankind most likely stumbled across the connection between sperm and pregnancy once they began the herding of animals. Early man probably noticed that when he kept the female animals separate from the males, no pregnancies occurred. The introduction of a male had obvious results. The parallels to human biology could not have gone unnoticed. Once the consequences of intercourse were realized, man's contraceptive experiments really began.

Why did women used to put dung into their vaginas?

Putting dung in the vagina is a rather repulsive thought. But such were the lengths to which women once went to prevent unwanted pregnancies. The Egyptians developed perhaps the most bizarre contraceptive techniques. One involved inserting a paste made with crocodile dung into the vagina. This was thought to block the passage of the sperm. (It may also have discouraged all but the most passionate suitors from penetration.)

Another Egyptian concoction contained a mixture of sodium carbonate (a salt) and honey or gum. Absorbent cloths soaked in honey with accacia tips were also employed. In ancient India, the vagina was anointed with honey and other mixtures, that included things like rock salt, oils, and clarified butter.

The ancients may not have realized it at the time, but gooey stuff really does retard sperm motility. Lactic acid, which is found in accacia tips, and salt, stop sperm dead in their tracks. In fact, lactic acid is still used in spermicides today. The Moslems used elephant dung as a contraceptive, which is even more acidic, and effective, than crocodile dung. The Greeks made ointments of olive and cedar oils, lead, and frankincense. The thickness of oils can slow down the motility of sperm.

The Jews believed that man, according to the Torah, was supposed to be fruitful and to multiply. Thus, birth control fell to the woman. Some of the Jewish methods were similar to the practices of other older cultures—herbal teas, sponges, and jumping up and down after intercourse. The Romans, meanwhile, put pepper in the vagina and recommended sneezing after intercourse to prevent pregnancy. During the Middle Ages people would spit three times into the mouth of a frog after intercourse.

All of the above mentioned contraceptive techniques more or less complicated the spontaneity of the "act" and most were rather disgusting to apply. They also placed all the burden of birth control squarely on the woman. It wasn't until much later in human history that male contraceptives came into vogue.

How did yams help revolutionize sex forever?

Ever heard of Russell Earl Marker? Neither have most people. He was a chemistry professor who worked with plant steroids in

Mexico in the 1930s. He knew that generations of Mexican women had been eating a wild yam—the barbasco root or *cabeza de negro*—for its contraceptive properties. Marker discovered that the steroid diosgenin, found in these yams, could be chemically altered to yield the human female sex hormone progesterone, from which progestin could be obtained.

Dr. Carl Djerassi synthesized norethindrone in Mexico City in 1951. It was the first orally active progestin. Gregory Pincus later used this knowledge to produce the first birth control pill. (See next question.)

What did International Harvester have to do with the invention of the pill?

The notion of oral birth control for women had few supporters in the first half of the twentieth century. It took the impetus of birth control advocate Margaret Sanger to encourage the development of a female contraceptive pill. Sanger was rebuffed in her attempts to get a pharmaceutical company to back her idea, so she began using her own money to fund research. In the early 1950s, she enlisted the help of her friend Katherine Dexter McCormick, heir to the International Harvester fortune.

McCormick was one of the first women to graduate from the Massachusetts Institute of Technology and was an ardent supporter of women's rights. In 1950, her husband Stanley died, making her a very wealthy woman. She asked her friend Sanger how she could use her money to contribute to contraceptive research.

Sanger took McCormick to see the work being done by two independent researchers at the Worcester Foundation for Experimental Biology: Gregory Pincus and Min Chueh Chang, who were experimenting with interrupting the fertility cycles of rabbits. They saw that progesterone could be used to mimic the condition of pregnancy in the body, which would inhibit ovulation. McCormick was so impressed that she began contributing between $150,000 to $180,000 a year toward the research project.

With her financial backing, they developed a contraceptive pill using the yam-based derivative progestin along with estrogen. In 1956, Catholic gynecologist Dr. John Rock conducted a small-scale clinical trial of the birth control pill on sixty volunteers. Pincus also ran successful large-scale tests on poor women in Puerto Rico and Haiti. In 1960, Searle Pharmaceuticals applied for FDA approval, and Enovid was born! Sanger, unfortunately, died in 1956, before seeing her dream realized.

At first, doctors only prescribed the Pill to married women. They somehow morally justified denying it to singles. Many women used fake wedding rings or marriage certificates to get around their prudish doctors. Clearer heads eventually prevailed and today, some ten million American women take the Pill (as it came to be known). The introduction of the Pill so liberated the sexuality of women that the rate of intercourse shot up dramatically.

What's going to replace the Pill?

The Pill is a modern miracle, but it probably won't last forever. A newer drug, DepoProvera®, may eventually surpass it in popularity. This drug has been available in ninety other countries since the 1970s, but was not granted FDA approval until 1992. Women are offered the same protection provided by the Pill simply by getting four injections a year—a much easier system to keep track of.

Will there ever be a male "Pill"?

Women complain about birth control (understandably, as they are the ones who get pregnant), but they have about a dozen contraceptive options. Men presently have one, excluding a vasectomy. A male version of the birth control pill would be a big seller and would help to take the onus away from the ladies.

Male hormonal-control pills are in the works that will suppress the production of sperm. This goal is trickier than it sounds. It is much harder to kill or suppress the millions of sperm that are produced each day than it is to control the release of one egg. These new drugs must fool the brain and pituitary gland into thinking that the sperm have already been produced. Another option is to render the sperm immobile with some kind of drug that affects the flagellum (sperm tail).

Scientists in Edinburgh, Scotland, are conducting trials of a hormone-releasing rod-shaped implant that is placed under the skin. The implant releases drugs that tell the brain to stop producing testosterone and sperm. Another implant is also needed to switch some testosterone back on again so the man doesn't lose his sex drive in the process. Reports say the drug is ninety-three percent effective. The doctor running the clinical trials says the side effects are "tiny" (no, that doesn't mean what you think it means!). It may be on the market in a few years.

Who are the "sperm police"?

It's not a who, but a what. Researchers at the Oregon Health Sciences University have discovered that a protein called ubiquitin is responsible for identifying defective sperm and labeling them so that they can be destroyed before ejaculation. Ubiquitin in the epididymis—the area near the testes where sperm are kept before ejaculation—attaches to the surface of defective sperm in many animals, including man. This discovery could help in the development of a male contraceptive pill.

Can spermicides be dangerous?

While effective at killing sperm, spermicides can damage the walls of the vagina if used to excess. Nonoxynol-9, the active ingredient in most spermicides, can cause the formation of very small holes in the vaginal lining. These holes can increase the chance of infection from an HIV-infected partner.

Another point to consider is that nonoxynol-9 can also kill some of the beneficial bacteria that inhabit and protect the vagina, making a woman more susceptible to outside bacterial infections. If you have a problem with yeast or urinary tract infections, you may want to steer clear of any products containing nonoxynol-9. Read the labels!

What ever happened to the Today Sponge?

The Today Sponge was invented by Bruce Vorhauer, Ph.D. in 1983. It went on to become many women's preferred choice of over-the-counter birth control, and accounted for twenty-eight percent of over-the-counter contraceptive sales. The sponge provided a physical barrier to sperm over the cervix, and also a chemical one. Each polyurethane sponge was impregnated (*pun unintended*) with the spermicide nonoxynol-9 and was eighty-five percent effective for up to twenty-four hours after insertion into the vagina.

The Today Sponge seemed to have a bright future. That was all to change in March 1994, when the Food and Drug Administration (FDA) did an inspection of the one plant that made the sponge. The FDA found bacterial contaminants in the water used to produce the sponge and shut the place down. The owners of the Today Sponge—Whitehall-Robbins Healthcare—decided it wasn't worth the trouble and expense to fix the problems at the plant and discontinued its production, much to the consternation of millions of American women (including Elaine, on the infamous "Spongeworthy" episode of the sitcom *Seinfeld*).

To the rescue came Gene Detroyer, CEO of Allendale Pharmaceuticals, Inc. They bought the Today Sponge from American Home Products in 1998 for $7 million and made plans to reintroduce it to the market. The FDA approved of the idea, as long as they made mention of the slight risk of Toxic Shock Syndrome and vaginal irritation on the packaging. Allendale met all the requirements, but the FDA has been dragging its feet about inspecting their plant and giving the final go-ahead to resume production. In March of 2003, the Today Sponge went on sale again in Canadian stores. Desperate American women have taken to ordering them online through Canadian Web sites. In the first ten weeks, Allendale sold some 300,000 sponges.

Before this, many American sponge users had switched to the Canadian-made Protectaid sponge. This sponge uses F-5 gel, a spermicide with three active ingredients—nonoxynol-9, benzalkonium chloride, and sodium chlorate—in low concentrations, so there is less of a risk of irritation of the cervix and vagina. Protectaid protects a woman for up to twelve hours and costs $14 for a pack of four. They can be ordered on the Web.

What one person did the most to undermine American birth control?

As the nineteenth century drew to a close, America became more sexually repressed. The one man who came to symbolize this extremism was Anthony Comstock. This man's sole mission in life was to rid America of anything he deemed obscene. He began his crusade by working with the YMCA to help suppress pornography. This led him to found the New York Society for the Suppression of Vice. He had supporters in Congress and a bill he pushed—the Comstock Act—was passed in 1873.

This act prohibited the mailing of any materials that were "lewd," "lascivious," "indecent," or "obscene." One big problem was that the law did not define any of these terms and it was left up to the discretion of the overzealous Comstock—who was appointed special postal agent—to screen the mail. He could basically open and seize any mail he wanted to. Publishers became afraid to mail any literature that wasn't "sanitized" and removed words or pictures from their material that might offend Comstock. By 1900, over 3,600 people had been arrested, 800,000 obscene pictures had been destroyed, and 98,000 articles on condoms seized thanks to him.

He was particularly opposed to birth control and really cracked down on the mailing of contraceptives and abortion aids or even information about birth control sent by doctors. Not only did this curtail any type of sex education and the availability of birth control; it also had deadly consequences. At least fifteen suicides were attributed to Comstock's harassments in the first five years after the passage of the Comstock Act. Many more followed during the thirty-seven years of his crusade.

One particular enemy of Comstock was a New York "woman's doctor," Madame Restell, who made her living through dispensing birth control and abortifacients. One day in 1878, he showed up at the sixty-seven-year-old lady's house and tricked her into selling him an abortifacient for his wife. Not wanting to face prison, she slit her throat.

The ironic thing about Comstock's anti-birth control mania was the fact that his own mother had fourteen children and died young. Rather than seeing his mother as a sufferer from the lack of available birth control, he believed she was a symbol of the fight against it.

What woman led the American crusade to legalize birth control?

One of the greatest crusaders to educate American women about birth control was social reformer Margaret Sanger. The term "birth control" didn't even exist until she coined it. As a nurse, she was deeply concerned about the terrible burden poor women had to endure as a result of the lack of readily available birth control or birth control information. She had also seen firsthand the horrors of illegal abortions. In 1914, she led a movement to bring women out of the sexual dark ages.

Sanger began writing birth control literature for public dissemination. In March 1914, Sanger published the first issue of *The Woman Rebel*, a radical feminist monthly that advocated "militant feminism," which included the right to practice birth control. This put her in Anthony Comstock's (remember him) doghouse. She was arrested and ended up fleeing to England to avoid prosecution.

On her way to England, Margaret ordered her friends to release 100,000 copies of the pamphlet *Family Limitation*, which gave explicit instructions on how to use contraceptives. This so enraged Comstock that he decided to go after Margaret's husband, William, who had remained in the States. He tricked Mr. Sanger into mailing some birth control literature to a postal agent. Mr. Sanger was promptly arrested and jailed.

Margaret returned to America in 1915 to stand trial, but when her five-year-old daughter died, the government dropped the case. In 1916, she opened the first birth control clinic in Brownsville, Brooklyn. Margaret started the American Birth Control League in 1921, which later joined with another group in 1942 to become the Planned Parenthood Federation of America. Later in her life, in the 1950s, Sanger helped to find the funding for the research that made the female contraceptive pill a reality.

While her progress was significant in educating American women, there were still laws on the books in some states prohibiting the mailing of birth control information up until 1970.

Other than cleaning, what else did women use Lysol for during the Depression?

During the late 1920s, American women had very little reliable information concerning birth control. Some were desperate enough to try anything, including disinfectants. Magazine ads promoted Lysol as a female douche as well as a household cleaner. Women used the cleaning product as a post-intercourse douche to kill sperm. Some used it to excess (if a little is good, a lot must be better) and ended up scalding their cervixes and vaginas. Thanks again, Mr. Comstock!

Why did the Arabs put stones into a camel's uterus?

Evidently, a pregnant camel is a foul and unruly beast, not good for much. The Arabs of Northern Africa somehow discovered that if you put a stone into the womb of a camel, it will not get pregnant. This curious practice, perhaps apocryphal, was the earliest version of an intrauterine device (IUD). However, it was Hippocrates who, over 2,500 years ago, first thought about applying this principle to women. Many substances were toyed with over the ages, including wood, glass, ivory, and gold.

It wasn't until 1909, however, that German physician Richard Richter came up with the first modern IUD, consisting of a ring of silkworm gut. Dr. Ernst Gräfenberg, of G-spot fame, introduced the first effective IUD in 1930. It consisted of silver rings and silkworm gut and had to be implanted by a doctor. Around the same time, a Japanese doctor came up with the gold and silver ring—the Ota ring. While these early modern IUDs were effective, they were found to cause infection and inflammation problems, so they lost their initial popularity.

Nothing much happened in IUD technology until the 1950s, when plastics came into the picture. The advantage to a plastic IUD was that it could spring back to its original shape after being stretched for insertion into the womb. The Lippes Loop and the Marguiles spiral were two early plastic IUDs.

The Lippes Loop, invented by Jack Lippes, a Buffalo, New York gynecologist in the early 1960s, was the first IUD with an attached tail, which made it easier to remove. It was an instant hit and is still popular worldwide today.

Why aren't IUDs more popular in the United States?

The problem with IUDs is that the bigger they are, the more effective they are. However, larger size means greater irritation, bleeding, and cramping. They also tend to get expelled by the uterus. This problem was addressed with the Dalkon Shield in the late 1970s.

Manufactured by A. H. Robbins of Richmond, Virginia, the Dalkon Shield was used by millions of women. Back in those days, the FDA did not regulate IUDs because they weren't classified as a drug. Hence, rigorous safety testing was not done. This was to prove disastrous for hundreds of thousands of women.

The Shield had side extensions that were supposed to prevent it from being expelled. However, the extensions made it difficult and painful to insert and remove. Worse yet, the string on the Shield was made of a porous material that acted as a wick, drawing bacteria up into the uterus. Many cases of severe pelvic infection resulted and some women even died. Others became pregnant on the Shield and miscarried their babies, often in the third to sixth months of their pregnancies. The product was pulled from the market in 1974 and eleven years later, the company filed for bankruptcy.

IUDs now have a plastic base, with copper or silver wound around it. T-shapes are the most common since they are more "womb-shaped" and are harder for the uterus to expel. The newest IUD, the Gynefix, has eliminated the plastic entirely to reduce its size. It is simply six copper tubing segments attached to a nylon thread.

IUD usage in the United States never rebounded from the Dalkon Shield debacle, although even the World Health Organization and the American Medical Association consider them one of the safest and most effective forms of reversible birth control available. While the IUD is the leading form of reversible birth control worldwide, American women have so many options that most don't have an interest in a product with a bad reputation.

How does an IUD work?

There are two types of IUDs available in the United States. Plastic IUDs with a copper coating on the arms, like ParaGard Copper T380 A (sounds like a sports car), can be left in place for ten years. Hormone-coated IUDs, like Merina and Progestasert, contain a small amount of progesterone and must be replaced after five years and one year, respectively. While both types are highly effective, no one is absolutely sure exactly how an IUD prevents pregnancy!

The old theory was that the presence of this "foreign" object in the body sets up an inflammatory response in the womb, which causes the production of extra white blood cells. These cells destroy bacteria and viruses. As long as the IUD remains in the body, white blood cells are present in the area of the IUD. Since sperm cells are also foreign bodies, the white blood cells would destroy them before they could fertilize the egg.

The latest studies, however, suggest that a copper IUD actually impedes the motility of the sperm and egg, preventing fertilization. Scientists are not sure how an IUD effects motility. It could be that chemicals released by the IUD cause the egg to move through the fallopian tube too quickly to become fertilized, or that the sperm is somehow immobilized.

Copper IUDs may also have an effect on the enzymes in the uteral lining, preventing implantation. Or they may cause an increased production of prostaglandins, which are responsible for causing the muscle of the womb to contract and the lining of the uterus to detach, causing bleeding. This may explain why some copper IUD users have heavier, more painful periods.

IUDs containing progesterone further act to thicken the cervical mucous, forming a barrier that stops the sperm from entering the uterus. They also make the lining of the womb very thin, stopping implantation. The Minera type of IUD has the added benefit of making a woman's periods lighter, and it is now also prescribed for this use as well.

Is all that clear? No? Well, the real answer may be a combination of some or all of the above. Just know that IUDs are one of the most reliable forms of reversible birth control, with a failure rate of less than one percent.

Did Casanova invent the diaphragm?

The great lover Giovanni Giacomo Casanova claims in his autobiography that he came up with the idea of the diaphragm. He used to insert half of a squeezed lemon into his lovers' vaginas to cover the cervix, acting as a rather crude from of cervical cap, or diaphragm. While the great lover may indeed have done this, he was hardly the first to think of it. Women had been putting barriers to sperm in their vaginas for centuries. Asian prostitutes put oiled paper discs over their cervixes, and the women of Easter Island employed algae and seaweed.

German gynecologist Fredrich Wilde created the first modern cervical cap in 1838. German women traditionally used discs of melted and molded beeswax to cover their cervixes. Wilde updated this custom with rubber "pessaries" custom made to fit each patient. Charles Goodyear, whose invention of vulcanized rubber transformed the world of condoms, also used his new material to manufacture rubber pessaries in the 1850s in Connecticut. They were sold through pharmacies, ostensibly as a support for the uterus or to hold medications in place.

By the time cervical caps and other modern forms of birth control caught on in the United States, the Comstock Act of 1873 came along and essentially made them impossible to get ahold of. (For more on Comstock, see pages 54–55.)

By the way, using half a squeezed lemon as a cervical cap wasn't such a bad idea. The rind does help to block sperm and the natural citric acids act as a spermicide.

How did 3 IN 1 Oil illegally help to make diaphragms available in the United States?

This is another little subplot involving Margaret Sanger and her ongoing battle with the Comstock Law and the United States Post Office.

While seeking refuge from Comstock in Holland in 1915, Sanger came across German diaphragms that were spring-loaded and fit tightly. Back in the United States, she was arrested in 1916 for telling women about their use. Sanger served a month in jail but never lost her resolve, even proselytizing to the other inmates during her incarceration. After her release, she solicited the help of her second husband, Noah Slee.

Slee was the owner of the company that made 3 IN 1 Oil. Sanger had Slee import diaphragms from makers in Holland and Germany to his factory in Montreal. From there, the contraceptives were shipped to New York, hidden inside 3 IN 1 boxes. Slee also helped Sanger acquire the lubricating jelly needed for the diaphragms. He obtained the German formula and began making the jelly illegally at his plant in Rahway, New Jersey. In 1925, Slee financed the founding of the Holland-Rantos Company, which manufactured the first American-made diaphragms.

Margaret Sanger was successful in fooling the postal inspectors, but birth control devices were still basically illegal. The fight wasn't over yet. In 1932, she had a Japanese colleague mail her a package of diaphragms, with the hope it would be confiscated by customs officials. It was. In a landmark case in the fight for legal birth control, *United States v. One Package,* Manhattan judge Augustus Hand, writing for the United States Court of Appeals, ruled the package could be delivered. This decision severely weakened the Comstock Law of 1873 and set in motion the legalization of the mailing of contraceptive information and supplies. (For more on Comstock and Sanger, see pages 54–56.)

By the 1940s, the medical world saw diaphragms as the most reliable form of birth control. However, with the increase in IUD usage and the invention of the Pill, cervical caps and diaphragms fell out of favor by the 1960s.

What is the number-one form of birth control in the United States?

Ten million women take the Pill, and a lot more would if it were covered by health insurance. Oddly enough, female sterilization *is* covered by most health insurers. As a result, eleven million American women have been sterilized, making it the number-one form of birth control. Harder on the body, but easier on the pocketbook.

Which pope wrote a hugely popular birth control recipe book?

Women around the world have been using herbal contraceptives for thousands of years. One of the best-selling books on herbal contraception, *Thesaurus Pauperum (Treasure of the Poor),* was written by a man who was to become pope. Peter of Spain, who wrote a recipe book on birth control and how to provoke menstruation, was elected Pope John XXI in 1276. Many of Peter's recipes have been tested by modern science and found to be effective to varying degrees.

CHAPTER FIVE

Put It On Before You Put It In!

Who is the condom named for?

The modern condom may be the key to safe sex and the best solution to the abortion issue, but this little latex wonder is totally taken for granted. Most of us don't even have a clue who invented it.

Supposedly, the condom gets its name from the apocryphal "Dr. Condom," who is said to have made penis sheaths for King Charles II of England, in the late seventeenth century. More likely, the name derives from the Latin word *condon*, meaning "receptacle." Either way, male sheaths were around long before the time of Charles II.

The earliest images of what are believed to be condoms were found on ancient 3,000-year-old Egyptian hieroglyphs. Whether they were ceremonial attire or functional prophylactics is open to debate. The ancient Chinese made condoms with oiled silk paper. It is rumored that Roman soldiers made them from the muscle tissue of their defeated enemies. By medieval times, syphilis was spreading quickly throughout Europe, and so was the use of the condom. The Italian anatomist Gabriello Fallopio (of fallopian tube fame) devised a linen sheath to prevent the spread of syphilis in 1564. It fit over the tip (glans) of the penis and was secured under the foreskin. The oldest condoms were discovered at the foundations of Dudley Castle near Birmingham, England, and date back to 1640. They were made of animal and fish intestines.

It wasn't until the 1700s that men seriously began to take responsibility for the disposition of their sperm and started wearing condoms. Before this time, condoms were worn more for disease prevention than for birth control. In the 1800s, condoms were made from animal intestines that were soaked in an alkaline solution, scraped, disinfected with vapor of burning brimstone, washed, inflated, dried, cut to approximately seven inches in length, and fitted with a ribbon for tightening at the open end. The Catholic Church wasn't too crazy about this prophylactic profusion and in 1826, Pope Leo XIII condemned their use. Despite his objections, condoms were here to stay.

What do condoms have in common with Goodyear tires?

Early condoms did not fit very well and were clumsy to put on. With Charles Goodyear's patenting of vulcanized (hardened) rubber in 1844, that would soon change. Vulcanization allowed the creation of rubber condoms, called, appropriately enough, "rubbers," which became very popular in the late 1870s. They were rather thick and somewhat reduced the man's pleasure, but they were tough and reusable (after washing). Rubber condoms were used until they cracked or tore. They sold for about five dollars a dozen. George Bernard Shaw was so impressed with them that he called rubbers "the best thing to come out of the Industrial Revolution." High praise indeed!

Rubbers were exhibited at the Philadelphia World Exposition in 1876. They gained great popularity and respectability due to the fact that their original packaging featured full-color portraits of Queen Victoria and Mr. Gladstone. By the 1930s, over 300 million were being sold a year.

With the development of liquid latex in the 1930s, latex condoms could be mass produced. Trojan brand was the first to do so. In 1950, one Stanley Penska patented the idea of putting a sperm reservoir on the tip of a condom, reducing leakage and breakage.

Today, about one million condoms are sold each day, with almost half of them purchased by women. Thirty percent of the time, it's the woman who puts the condom on her partner.

What army had the highest rate of venereal disease in World War I?

The one with the most prudish government, of course. American troops returned from Europe with the highest venereal disease rate of any country's army. We can thank a certain Mr. Comstock for this sad fact. In 1873, he helped push a bill through Congress that essentially outlawed birth control. (For more on this, see pages 54–56.)

Thus, when the United States entered World War I in 1917, the American soldier's kit was the only one that did not come with condoms.

Instead, the military preached abstinence. Troops were told that the only women who wanted to sleep with them were the enemy. They were instructed that VD was a worse weapon than the Kaiser's bullets. Because of such a foolish approach to military sex, over seven million man days were lost during the war to sexually transmitted diseases.

An underground condom business flourished in the United States, however. Consequently, the illegal condoms that were available were of poor quality and had a sixty-percent failure rate. It wasn't until the end of the 1920s that condoms could be legally manufactured in America. By World War II, the country's "morality" and the government loosened up and condoms were dutifully supplied at taxpayer expense.

Officials worried that American GIs might return home from the war with diseases and infect their wives. During World War II, monthly shipments of condoms reached fifty million. Each soldier received eight per month. Military training films promoted the use of condoms with the slogan "Don't forget, put it on before you put it in." Women in the military (WACs and WAVs), however, were denied the same sexual consideration. It is estimated that up to eighty-five percent of American GIs had sex while overseas, fathering tens of thousands of illegitimate children in Europe.

An illustration of how much the military's philosophy on sex has changed over the years: In 1998 the Pentagon spent $50 million on Viagra for the troops and veterans.

Do condoms come in sizes?

For years condom manufacturers assumed that one size really did fit all. Most manufacturers sold condoms that were either fifty-two centimeters or fifty-four centimeters wide when laid flat. Bigger guys may need this much room but some guys are smaller or just prefer a tighter fit. The Durex Close Fit condom, at forty-nine millimeters, is narrower and offers "a firmer hold and potentially less slippage," making it safer and more comfortable for some men. The Close Fit is currently being marketed in Britain. The fifty-four millimeter condom is the biggest seller in Europe, but the company thinks the Close Fit will be a big seller in the Far East, where men tend to be more diminutive. Regular-sized condoms should fit most guys, however.

A Swedish condom maker, RFSU, sells condoms in three sizes and a Condometer as a sizing aid, so men can make sure they have a proper fit. The three sizes offered are the Mamba "Snugger" Condom, a narrow-fitting condom that is 175 millimeters long and 51 millimeters wide; the Birds & Bees Textured Condom, at 185 millimeters x 52 millimeters; and the Okeido Extra Large, at 190 millimeters x 53 millimeters. For you real "slim jims" out there, RFSU has the Pasante Trim Condom that is just forty-nine millimeters wide. You can send away to the company for free sample condoms and a Condometer, or visit their Web site.

When did polyurethane condoms debut?

We had been relying on the latex condom since the 1930s until, finally, someone came up with a better model. A British company, London International Group, parent company of Durex and the largest manufacturer of condoms in the world, began to market a new polyurethane condom in the 1990s.

These Saran Wrap spin-offs look wrinkly and clear, kind of like a plastic bag. They are two times thinner than latex condoms, and thus offer greater sensitivity and better heat transfer. They also eliminate the problem of latex allergies and can be used with oil-based lubricants that would break down a latex condom. They also require less lubrication, as they are almost friction free.

Polyurethane condoms have become quite popular. However, one study found that polyurethane condoms come off or break at a rate of 8.5 percent during intercourse or withdrawal, as compared to 1.5 percent with latex. Perhaps this is because they don't fit as tightly as latex condoms. So enjoy the poly condoms, but be careful, especially when withdrawing.

Is there a faster way to put on a condom?

Many people avoid condoms because they feel that they are "passion killers." What's more awkward than stopping in the middle of a romantic interlude, flipping on the light, and fumbling around with an uncooperative rubber? Well despair no more; the condom applicator is here. Instead of the clumsy thirty to forty seconds it usually takes to put on a condom, the new condom applicator can have you fully sheathed and ready to go in just three seconds! Or so claims the maker.

The applicator was developed by a South African entrepreneur named Willem van Rensburg, who has yet to market this marvel. His funding came from South African life insurer Metropolitan, who is eager to help encourage the use of condoms in a country with one of the world's highest HIV/AIDS rates. According to a Metropolitan spokesman, the applicator is made of polyethylene and comes in the same package as the condom. To use it, you bend the package and it splits open. You then slide the condom onto the penis and the applicator pops off. Sounds easy, doesn't it? Nothing is ever that easy.

In which country do people use the most condoms?

According to a German sex study, eighty-two percent of sixteen to forty-five-year-olds in Thailand always use condoms when having sex with a casual partner. (Considering all the prostitution there, it's a good idea.) Other countries use condoms in the following order—France: sixty-nine percent, United States: fifty-six percent, Italy: forty-eight percent, England: forty percent, Spain:

thirty-six percent, Germany: thirty-two percent, Canada and Poland: less than twenty-five percent.

Can wearing a condom make sex last longer?

Yes. A condom reduces the pleasurable sensations brought on by intercourse and can give a man greater stamina. The thicker the condom, the better. However, more help is here. New condoms are available that are lined with the anesthetic benzocaine. The numbing effect of this drug can prolong sex for ninety percent of the men who try them.

In 2001, the makers of Trojan-brand condoms introduced the Extended Pleasure condom, America's first desensitizing condom. It has a climax-control lubricant, containing four percent benzocaine, in the tip. Not only will it help extend the lovemaking of all sexually active couples, but it will also benefit the nearly thirty percent of couples who identify premature ejaculation as a problem.

Over twenty-one million of these condoms have already been sold. At a suggested retail price of $8.99 for a box of twelve, it could be well worth the trip to the store.

What should you do if your condom breaks?

If you are one of the minority of people who use a condom to prevent pregnancy, your worst sex nightmare is the broken condom! The chances of a condom breaking during intercourse are about one in one hundred. If you are unfortunate enough to have a condom break in the heat of passion, stay calm, all is not lost. The chances of pregnancy from unprotected intercourse are roughly one in three. If you want to decrease these odds, try the following.

Hopefully you were using spermicidal condoms. The spermicide may kill any sperm that have leaked out. To be safe, though, insert several applications of spermicidal foam into the vagina quickly, before the active sperm can get through the cervix. Douching, however, is not a good idea. Instead of cleansing you, douching can actually push the sperm past the cervix.

Are German men too small for the European Union?

Believe it or not, the European Union (EU) has established size guidelines for condoms. The recommended condom size for the "average" European penis doesn't sit too well with Germany. They contend that the EU has overestimated the average penis size by twenty percent.

A sampling of German penises found that they were too small for the recommended EU condom size. A German's average penis length is 14.48 centimeters, with a width of 3.95 centimeters. That is much smaller than the EU condom length of 17 centimeters and width of 5.6 centimeters. Of course the Germans argue that they are not any smaller than the rest of Europe, but that the EU has been overgenerous in its calculations.

When do condoms turn bright green?

When they're filled with dye. A new kind of condom that changes color when punctured may be on the market someday.

The United States Patent Office has issued a patent for a three-layer condom that has a dye in the middle layer. If a tear should occur and the dye is exposed to the air, the condom color will change to bright green or purple.

If and when this product ever comes out, it will be immediately apparent to even the most impatient condom user whether or not the sheath is safe to use. Right now, a tiny hole in a condom can easily be missed.

Can condoms be used as life preservers?

This story sounds too weird to be true, but it actually was reported on the major wire services during the summer of 1996. A man was saved from drowning by a pair of condoms. Apparently, he fell off of a pleasure boat somewhere near the coast of Australia. Luckily, the thirty-six-year-old had some condoms in his wallet. He supposedly blew up two of them and used them as flotation devices. After ten hours in the water, he was rescued.

However, it's not recommended that you pack condoms instead of life jackets on your next boat outing.

What is a female condom?

The male condom has been around for a long time. Recently, a female version has come along. The Reality Female Condom is a soft, loose-fitting polyurethane sheath that is 17 centimeters long and 7.8 centimeters in diameter. There are two rings, one on each end. The ring on the closed end of the device is flexible and is inserted into the vagina, holding the condom in place. The ring on the open end remains outside the vagina and covers the vulva. The inside of the sheath is coated with a silicone-based lubricant. Additional lubricant, for the outside, is provided with the condom.

The female condom can be inserted up to eight hours before intercourse and is as good as the male condom, in terms of STD and pregnancy prevention, when *properly* used. Its polyurethane is a thin, strong plastic that transfers heat well and is less likely to break than latex. Oil-based products will not break it down and it stores better than a latex condom. So if you choose this form of protection, there is no need for the male version. In fact, male and female condoms should never be used together, as they will rub against one another, causing slippage or displacement.

Initially introduced in 1993, the female condom had a high failure rate of twenty-one percent among users in the first year. The company says, used *properly*, the failure rate is closer to five percent. Another drawback is an annoying squeaking or rustling sound that can occur during intercourse. Add to that a $3 price tag and you can see why it's not too popular.

CHAPTER SIX

Unmentionables

Who invented the bra?

Several people claim to have invented the brassiere, but it has been around since ancient times. Women athletes in ancient Greece and Rome held their breasts in soft leather straps that tied in the back. These garments were designed to minimize the bosom rather than support it. Other than the athletes, Roman women let their breasts swing free under their loose-fitting tunics.

The modern bra didn't start to gain recognition until 1913, when New York socialite Mary Phelps Jacobs fashioned a backless garment to support her breasts, using two handkerchiefs, a piece of ribbon, and a length of cord. She hadn't set out to revolutionize the world of women's apparel; she just couldn't wear a corset with the new backless sheer gown she had purchased.

Mary was very pleased with her creation, and she started making them for her friends. Response was so positive that Mary filed for a patent. In November 1914, she was granted a patent for the "backless bra." Mary didn't have much luck making and marketing her invention and later sold her patent to the Warner Brothers Corset Company of Bridgeport, Connecticut for a mere $1,500—a deal she would live to regret.

But did Mary Phelps Jacobs actually invent the modern bra? Not really. Several other patents had been issued before Mary's. Some even had cups. She was just the first to do anything with the idea. Far from being a true breast-support device, as is the modern bra, Mary's contraption was more of a breast flattener, and she described it as a "chest wrap."

During a trip to France after World War I, Mary happened upon the word *brassiere*, which was used to describe any type of upper body support that had arm straps. Mary fancied the term and had it attached to her creation. The word was later shortened to "bra."

Who came up with cup sizes?

Cup sizes were the concept of Ida Rosenthal, a Russian Jewish immigrant to America. She and her husband William started the Maidenform Company in 1922. In the 1920s, during the age of the flappers, women preferred the flat-chested look. They would bind their breasts to achieve a somewhat boyish appearance. Ida was a woman of ample bosom and felt that it was just a matter of time before big breasts would come back into vogue.

Being a seamstress and dressmaker, Ida decided to come out with a line of sized bras that would lift and highlight each woman's natural assets according to her particular breast size. She settled on dividing women's breasts into the four cup sizes we are familiar with today—A, B, C, and D. It sounds obvious enough, but no one had done it before Ida.

Warner Brothers adopted the sizing system in 1935 and later tweaked it, adding the AA and DD sizes. (They also brought out the all-elastic bra around this time, which better showed off a woman's curves.)

Beginning in 1949, Maidenform ran a series of ads, shocking for the day, featuring confident, aggressive women wearing their Maidenform bras. The ads, which ran for twenty years, had women in different public situations wearing nothing above the waist but a bra. This was the ad campaign that coined the famous slogan "I Dreamed I Stopped Traffic in My Maidenform Bra." The reason the company got away with these scandalous ads was that since the girl was supposed to be *dreaming* about being undressed, it was okay.

What is the average American breast size?

The average American bustline is a hair under thirty-six inches. The most common bra size sold is 34B or 36B. Women wear cup sizes in the following proportions—A: fifteen percent, B: forty-four percent, C: twenty-eight percent, and D: ten percent, with AA, AAA, and DD making up the remaining three percent. However, the Intimate Apparel Council in New York reports that up to seventy-five percent of American women are wearing the wrong size bra. Most women are squeezing into a size that is too small. According to the council, the average breast size has increased in the last decade from 34B to 36C. Why the recent blossoming bosom? Factors include better nutrition, increases in exercise, and the boom in breast augmentation. They recommend that you get remeasured once a year. They also recommend putting your bra on the right way, by bending over first, to ensure a better fit.

Also, as many as half of all women have one breast that is larger than the other. The bra makers haven't addressed this issue yet. (Different size cups on the same bra. There's a million-dollar idea, folks!)

What actress had a bra custom-designed for her by Howard Hughes?

Hollywood has always had a great influence on American fashion. During the 1940s and 1950s, starlets were so emulated that they even had an affect on the kinds of bras that were in vogue. Lana Turner, for example, popularized the pointy, cone-shaped bra that was accentuated when worn under a tight sweater. She became known as America's "Sweater Girl." These brassieres achieved their cone shapes through close circular stitching in the cups. The point on these bras became so sharp by the 1950s that they would stick through the sweater's wool material.

The actress with perhaps the most famous boobs of the 1940s was Jane Russell. So big and jiggly were her breasts that they presented a problem when casting her in movies. The censors couldn't handle Jane's breasts bouncing around on film. To the rescue came her lover, producer Howard Hughes. As well as being the country's richest man, he was a movie mogul and engineer (he designed and built the world's largest airplane—the Spruce Goose). Putting his engineering skills to work, he minutely measured Jane's breasts with a caliper, determined the stress factors at work, and constructed the perfect support for her—the cantilevered bra. It also lifted and separated her breasts to boot.

Jane wore the new bra in the 1947 movie, *The Outlaw*. Howard's creation was a stunning success. Jane's bosom protruded straight out with nary a jiggle. One critic remarked, "Her breasts hung over the picture like a thunderstorm." The movie helped to bring cleavage out of the cinematic closet.

What article of lingerie is men's favorite?

A 2002 Maidenform survey revealed that men's favorite lingerie item is the thong. The women surveyed, however, fancied the bra as the sexiest part of their wardrobe. (The garter belt, which was more popular in older days, ranked at the bottom of the sexy lingerie list.)

Whereas only the women rated the brassiere tops, both sexes agreed on who had the best breasts to put in a bra. Halle Berry was thought by men and women to have the most perfect breasts. One footnote: The average woman owns about ten bras, of which she only wears six. The average bra only lasts for about 180 days of use.

Why did women's breasts used to explode on airplanes?

Actually, their breasts didn't explode; their bras did. For a while in the 1950s, women could buy bras equipped with inflatable plastic air bags, attached to a little hand pump. The wearer could inflate her bosom to the desired size at will. It was a nifty idea, but had a couple of drawbacks. The air bags might leak slowly, leaving uneven breasts. More embarrassing, they were prone to exploding on high-altitude flights, due to the poorly pressurized planes of the era.

What are "Nippets"?

There may be times when a woman wants to conceal her nipples, such as when wearing lingerie, a swimsuit, a sheer top or bra, or no bra at all. The answer for these occasions are "Nippets." These are padless nipple-concealment strips that are placed over the nipples, much like Band-Aids, which stop the nipples from protruding through clothing. Nippets can be very useful when wearing certain tops in the workplace. They can be left on for several days and can even be worn in the shower or while swimming.

What article of women's intimate apparel was once used to make airplane tires?

In 1930, DuPont chemist Walter Carothers mixed coal tar, water, and air and came up with a new "miracle fiber"—nylon. Not knowing what to do with this new material, nylon was first used to make fishing line. It wasn't until 1939 that the first pair of nylon stockings made their debut at the World's Fair in New York. (The "ny" part of nylon is in honor of the NY World's Fair.) "Nylons," as they were called, were touted as impossible to snag or develop a run. One pair would last forever. While these claims were clearly bogus, women still went wild for them and the days of silk stockings were numbered.

May 15, 1940 was declared Nylon Day, when the first nylon stockings went on sale nationwide for $1.25 a pair. Women lined up outside stores hours before they opened and stocks immediately sold out. The New York allotment of 72,000 pairs was gone in eight hours. Thirty-six million pairs were bought in the next seven months. The only thing preventing bigger sales was DuPont's inability to keep up with the demand. Nylons dramatically reduced the silk stocking market, and that was just fine with millions of women. Happy times, regrettably, were soon to end.

With the advent of World War II, nylon stocking production was slashed, as nylon was needed for the war effort to make parachutes, tents, and ropes. Existing nylons were collected and melted down to make airplane tires. The few pairs still available appeared on the black market and were very expensive, about $10 a pair.

Why did women used to draw black lines up the backs of their legs?

The great nylon shortage of World War II took its toll on American women. So attached had they become to the recently introduced nylon stockings that they could not bear to let them go. They either took to silk stockings again or tried to make their legs *look* like they were wearing nylons.

Because nylon was easier to manufacture in sheets, nylon stockings were stitched together at the backs of the legs. Far from being an unsightly seam, this line became one of the sexiest looks the leg has ever seen. In order to create the illusion of nylons, many women colored their bare legs dark beige and drew dark lines up the back with an eyebrow pencil.

What happened to stockings?

It was the introduction of the miniskirt that had a lot to do with the demise of stockings. One major problem with stockings was that they had to be held up by girdle snaps or garter belts. The latter may be sexy, but both means of attachment are less than ideal. However, women lived with the annoyance. When skirts started rising in the 1960s, things began to change. In 1965, super model Twiggy made the miniskirt the hot new fashion. To prevent immodesty, a new type of hosiery was needed.

Pantyhose were just a natural upward extension of nylon stockings. They had been introduced in 1959 by Glen Raven Mills of North Carolina, but were worn primarily by theatrical people and dancers. The miniskirt was just what the pantyhose makers were waiting for. Once women started wearing pantyhose with their shorter skirts, they found them so convenient that stockings have never recovered since. By 1969, pantyhose had captured a seventy-percent market share.

Pantyhose not only killed off stockings, but girdles as well. Introduced in the 1920s as a less severe body-shaping device than the corset, girdles shaped the abdomen and buttocks, and were a convenient place to attach the top of the stockings.

Whatever happened to the corset?

Corsets have been around, in one form or another, since ancient times. Even the men in ancient Crete appear to have constricted their waists in corset-like garments. However, we can thank Catherine de Medici of high heel fame (see pages 82–84) with helping popularize them in their more modern form. She banned thick waists in her court and ordered the ladies-in-waiting to cinch their waists to no bigger than thirteen inches (apparently she was quite particular), thus forcing these women to wear corsets, which squeezed in the waist and pushed up the breasts. In was in her court that the metal framework corset appeared.

The corset remained hugely popular through the Victorian era but saw the beginning of its end in the United States when America entered the Great War in 1917. The government told women to give up corsets as the military needed the metal for the war effort. Some 28,000 tons of metal were thus saved. That's a lot of corsets.

The 1920s brought the loosely dressed flappers. Curves were out and thin was in. Larger women could help achieve this look with a light corset, or girdle, and bandeau—a band-shaped wrap that minimized the bosom. When elastic undergarments and bras caught on in the 1930s, the corset was laid to rest as an everyday garment.

However, some people, men and women alike, wear them today for sex play or other uses. They can be found at specialty shops and online if you are interested.

When did girdles become popular?

A girdle is an elastic garment designed to shape and smooth a woman's figure from the waist to the thighs. From the 1920s to the late 1970s, girdles were almost universally worn by women.

Most fashion historians believe the girdle was first created by French fashion designer Paul Poiret in 1910. He revolutionized clothing design by placing much less emphasis on the waist and focusing on a closer fit around the hips and buttocks. These designs were not appropriate for a corset, so a new tight-fitting foundation garment was needed. A woman had to be smooth and sleek if she were going to wear the new fashions that were evolving, so Poiret created this radical new undergarment.

Girdles, and, later, panty girdles (girdles with legs) became quite popular in the 1920s as a less severe foundation than the corset. They also had the added benefit of shaping the abdomen and buttocks.

The big innovation in girdle design came about in the 1930s, with the invention (by Dunlop Rubber chemists) of an elasticized latex rubber thread that could be used in fabrics. This new thread, "Lastex," was used to make the "Gossard Complete" girdle. It fastened with hooks and bars, and its elastic panels provided figure control. Some later girdles, in the late 1950s and early 1960s, were made of cream rubber that was covered with little ventilation holes for evaporation. These girdles left an imprint of tiny dots all over the wearer's bottom!

As fashions changed and females became more "liberated," the girdle started to lose popularity among younger women. The girdle came to be seen as old ladies' underwear. Today, girdles are made of interwoven nylon and Lycra spandex and are lighter and easier to wear than their stiffer, heavier predecessors. Girdles are making something of a comeback, although they are now called a host of other names, none of which conjure up the dowdy image of the word "girdle." Ads use terms such as "body-briefer," "control bottom," "long-line slimmer," "shaper," "shapesuit," or "sports brief" to encourage a new generation of women to embrace this updated undergarment from the time of their grandmothers.

What lady has the world's thinnest waist?

While the corset may have fallen out of favor as an everyday garment, it still has its proponents. One such worshiper of the corset is American Cathie Jung. She has been wearing a corset every day for twelve years now. The Guinness Book of World Records lists her as having the smallest waist in the world. It is said to be no bigger than that of a regular-size jar of mayonnaise. So fond is she of corsets that she owns around one hundred of them, and wears one twenty-four hours a day to keep her wasp-like figure.

Are there pantyhose for men?

Many women presently are going for the bare-leg look so the hosiery industry is targeting a new potential market: men. A women's wholesale hosiery company, G. Lieberman & Sons Ltd., sells pantyhose made specifically for men. They have a front fly opening and are made of nylon and Lycra spandex. The new male hosiery is called ActivSkin and can be bought online.

The main consumers of ActivSkin are athletes but the product is also being sold for work and leisure wear. The company claims that some men like pantyhose because they keep their legs warm while allowing perspiration to evaporate. They also offer support, stimulate circulation, prevent chafing, and are comfortable to wear. You'd probably find disagreement from most women on that last point.

When did women start wearing panties?

We take underwear for granted today but in the not-so-distant past, people didn't wear any. Noblewomen may have worn petti-coats and corsets, but even they wore nothing between their legs.

For most of history, people were quite unsanitary. Few had access to clean running water and laundering was almost unheard of. Most common people wore the same clothes for up to a year, unwashed. Underpants would quickly become soiled and unwearable. In the case of women, dirty underpants would be a breeding ground for yeast and other infections. A vagina exposed to the air would remain drier and cooler, thus inhibiting infection.

Also, by going "au naturel," it was very easy for a lady in a dress to relieve herself, simply by squatting at any convenient spot. Underpants would have made things complicated. If one did wear undergarments, it was to provide warmth in cold climates and the garments worn were generally long stockings, tights, or tunics.

Amelia Bloomer was the first woman of note to wear undergarments. In 1850, she wore loose-fitting ankle-length pants under her knee-high skirt as she toured the country preaching about women's liberation. Amelia inspired some other women to wear these trousers, called "bloomers," but they really didn't gain widespread acceptance.

We can thank the Victorians for making underclothes popular. Because of their prudishness, they frowned upon going "naked" under the clothes of the day, which had lighter, tighter-fitting fabrics. The doctors of the era warned both sexes against catching a chill down there and thus becoming infected with some horrible contagion. By the time that Louis Pasteur developed his germ theory in the 1880s, the general public had already developed quite a phobia about germs and cleanliness. As more people had the means to wash clothing, the wearing of underclothes became the sanitary thing to do.

Underwear was worn primarily for health reasons. Fashion and comfort didn't enter into the equation. Early underclothes were white, starched, and ironed. They could be rather uncomfortable and itchy and the drawstrings that held them up were bulky. Thanks to the introduction of cheap elastic waistbands in 1900 and the lighter, silkier fabrics that would follow, the modern panty was born.

While the masses were now "protected" by their underwear from the scourge of disease, all were not so happy. Many men missed the time of women walking around with nothing on under their dresses. Although it didn't happen often, in the old days a fellow had a slight chance of catching a glimpse of a lady's nether regions if she bent or fell over.

One of the most famous movie scenes of all-time is when Marilyn Monroe's dress blows up, exposing her panties. The scene was quite risqué for its time. In real life, Marilyn never wore panties on or off the set. That would have been even more exciting.

When did men start wearing briefs?

Before the turn of the century, men wore underwear strictly for warmth. Men's underpants were long and baggy knit-wool garments with buttons on the fly. They were worn with a knit-wool top from one Saturday night bath to the next. The button fly made relieving oneself somewhat inconvenient. The buttons were also uncomfortable on the crotch and tended to break when laundered in the hand-cranked wringers of the time. Men then began wearing red wool, one-piece union suits that had strategically placed buttonless flaps. These, however, were criticized as a "humpy, lumpy, creasy, baggy proposition, chafing and cutting your nethers." That was to change with the introduction of the X-shaped fly, in 1909.

The X-shaped fly was the brain child of Horace Greeley Johnson, a supervisor at the Cooper Underwear Company, of Kenosha, Wisconsin, forerunner of Jockey International Inc. His innovation, called the "Kenosha Klosed Krotch," featured two knit pieces that formed an overlapped X that could be drawn apart when required. It resulted in a single piece of cloth over the sensitive male area. This design has changed little over the years.

In 1934, the company further modernized undershorts when they began selling the white cotton Jockey brief. The design was copied from a French men's bathing suit that had been popular a year earlier. This sleek white brief was named "Jockey" because it sounded athletic.

What do Scottish men wear under their kilts?

Today, seven out of ten Scotsmen still abstain from wearing underpants with their kilts. When asked why, the traditional

Scotsman's reply may be, "Nothing is worn beneath the kilt, it's all in perfect working order" (whatever that means). The Scottish kilt, which may look like a plaid skirt for men, wasn't created as a fashion statement. It was a multipurpose garment made from a large rectangle of cloth, fifteen feet long by five feet wide, called a *philabeg*. It was folded lengthwise, wrapped around the waist, and then belted in place. The remainder of the cloth was thrown over the shoulder and pinned. This skirtlike apparel gave the men of the Highlands unrestricted movement of their limbs while traversing its rugged terrain. The kilts of old were very versatile, since they could be pulled over the head during inclement weather or used as a blanket. While we may think of a kilt as a skirt, women still don't wear them.

Today, kilts are pleated skirts with matching *plaids*, or blanketlike mantles that are worn over the left shoulder and fastened with a brooch. Included in this festive outfit is a purselike pouch, called the *sporran*, and knee-high stockings.

Modern kilt makers have finally added a pocket to the pleated skirt, so the active Scotsman has a place to keep his cell phone. A decorative pin is usually worn so the kilt will not come open and reveal the wearer's undergarments, or lack thereof. Those who *do* wear something to keep them warm usually choose boxers with a tartan print.

Who was Frederick of Hollywood?

Frederick N. Mellinger was a horny American GI in a foxhole during World War II. He dreamed of selling a line of sexy women's lingerie when he returned to the States, like those popular in France. American lingerie of the time was utilitarian and plain. Even a black bra would have been considered scandalous. He wanted American women to wear something that made them feel sexier and that men would find exciting as well.

Mellinger survived the war and started Frederick's of Fifth Avenue upon his return to New York in 1946. To increase business, he moved his operation to Hollywood, where many starlets were already wearing sexy French lingerie, and where his "racy" undergarments would meet with greater acceptance. Frederick's of Hollywood went on to introduce many new styles of lingerie to the American woman.

Mellinger is credited with selling the first push-up bra in the United States, the "Rising Star," in the early 1950s. Other Frederick's innovations include the front-close bra, bras with padded shoulder straps, and padded girdles. But perhaps the most erotic article of underwear he introduced to America was the thong panty in 1981. Today, Frederick's sells tens of thousands of them a year, in over twenty-five styles. The most popular thong style, worldwide, is the "Rio."

Frederick's best-selling bra is their Water Bra, which debuted in 1998. Its push-up "padding" is filled with rosewater and oil, giving it a more natural look and feel. The Water Bra is said to add a full cup size and is leak-proof. The Hollywood Kiss is another unique Frederick's bra. It has a "wishbone" construction with all-around wiring that creates a "kissing cleavage." (You'll have to use your imagination on this one.)

Frederick's of Hollywood, formed by the randy soldier, now has 200 retail shops in about forty states, a huge mail-order catalog business, and an online shopping site. Unfortunately, the company incurred heavy debts and was forced to file for Chapter 11 bankruptcy protection. It is now owned by the investment firm Wilshire Partners.

Who invented high heels?

It is estimated that ten percent of the men in the world entertain some sort of foot fetish. The number-one article of women's apparel men most fetishize is the high heeled shoe. Of all the garments a woman can wear, perhaps no other item adds to her sex appeal more than a pair of high heeled shoes. But what makes this uncomfortable accessory so appealing to the opposite sex?

Unlike other articles of clothing that just look nice on their own or highlight a particular physical trait of the wearer, high heels actually change and enhance several erotic areas on the body. So who would start this craze for shoes that women find uncomfortable and men find irresistible—a man, right? Wrong. Actually, high heels came into vogue during the sixteenth century, and you can thank the Italian-born noblewoman and fashion trendsetter Catherine de Medici, wife of Henry II of France, for their rise to popularity. She was quite small and had specially designed high shoes made for her. The trend soon swept the aristocracy. They must have been somewhat ungainly, as many of these women had to be supported by attendants when trying to walk.

When did high heels catch on in America?

While European aristocracy enjoyed high heels centuries ago, this fashionable shoe didn't appear in the United States until the mid-1800s. However, it wasn't some European blue blood who bought high heels across the Atlantic, but a common hooker.

A French prostitute brought several pairs with her to a high-class brothel in New Orleans. The madame found that the male customers were willing to pay more for this high-heeled French girl and ordered pairs for all the girls in the house. Word spread to the other brothels in town and soon all the classy hookers wore them. Men then began to order them for their wives. All this shoe buying didn't escape the notice of a Massachusetts shoe factory, which began domestically producing high heels in 1880.

Why are high heels still popular?

What is the special effect that high heels have on those who wear them? By pushing up the heels and essentially forcing a woman to walk on tiptoe, high heels alter the overall posture and position of the body parts. They simultaneously tilt the buttocks, tighten up the calf muscles, and arch the back, which pushes out the breasts and causes the woman to walk erect with swaying hips. All these changes play on the natural strutting walk women subconsciously adopt when courting a man. Needless to say, men find these body modifications quite fascinating. All in all, not a bad return for a little discomfort. No wonder they are as popular today as they were 400 years ago.

Why was the bustle once popular?

It seems that men have always admired a nicely proportioned female bottom. The one fashion statement that took this accentuation of the derriere to the extreme was the bustle. At the end of the eighteenth century, a padded or wire device, called a bustle, was worn over a woman's posterior to support her skirt.

Between 1869 and 1875, bustles increased in size and became something of a fashion craze. The bustles of this time supported accentuated drapes of cloth on the hips and backside. They were softer and had a fuller front than later bustles. Not only did they enhance the look of a lady's bottom, they also helped protect it from the attention of unwanted hands.

Between 1875 and 1883, slimmer silhouettes came into vogue and the bustle fell out of favor.

The bustle was reintroduced to the fashion world in 1883, and it came back in a big way. This second version of the bustle had a straw cushion sewn into the skirt, with a series of steel half-hoops inside the skirt's lining that went down to the ground. This had the effect of throwing the skirt out almost horizontally in the rear. So enormous were some of these bustles that they could support a tray of tea! The newer bustle also had less fabric in front, providing a flatter, tighter fit that was rather revealing.

Like many fashion fads, the second coming of the bustle was also short-lived. By 1893, it had given way to just a pad as women's silhouettes began to take on a more hourglass form.

When did thin become in?

In cultures and time periods in history where food was in short supply, only the affluent could afford to eat well. In these settings, fat women were usually found to be desirable. Their bulk showed that they were well fed and healthy. For most of history, Rubenesque women have been considered desirable. Obese women have always been prized in parts of Africa and many girls there are still sent to "fat farms" to be plumped up.

In times of abundant food like our present-day Western society, thin is in. Being thin shows that a woman has the time, resources, and desire to exercise and take care of herself. Fat women are thought to be less healthy, or even slovenly.

When did we become sun worshipers?

The same sort of rationale goes for tans. In past times, women powdered their faces with ceruse and chalk to appear white and gaunt. This implied that they were affluent enough to be ladies of leisure, kept indoors, as opposed to the working classes who had to toil in the sun. Wide-brimmed bonnets and parasols helped ensure a light complexion when ladies had to venture out-of-doors.

Today, the opposite rationale is true. A tan symbolizes a woman who has enough leisure time to lay out in the sun or engage in healthful athletic activities. It is the working-class women that are cooped up in factories or cubicles, devoid of sunlight.

It wasn't until the 1920s that tans replaced lily-white skin as a fashion statement. When revered fashion mogul Coco Chanel returned from a pleasure cruise on the Duke of Westminster's yacht sporting a tan, suddenly everyone had to have one. Now people want a tan all year long. Witness the boom in tanning salons in the late twentieth century. An all-year tan suggests one who is affluent enough to take trips to exotic locales in the dead of winter.

When were blue veins popular?

Today, women and men will spend thousands of dollars to get rid of varicose, or bluish, veins. Such was not the case in ancient Egypt. The Egyptians were compulsive about the cleanliness of their bodies. The affluent ones bathed three times a day and perfumed the entire body. Their wardrobe preference was a translucent fabric draped over the body in various ways. The women may or may not have covered their breasts. Those who were covered by the sheer fabric were often not well hidden. One feature that made a lady particularly proud of her bosom was the presence of dark blue veins. These were also quite desirable on the legs, which were often exposed. To enhance this sign of beauty, women would deepen the bluish color of their veins with dye.

When did nipple rings come into vogue?

Young people today think that any fad of our time is always something new and different. Although some people today may be taking body piercing to an extreme, nipple rings are actually nothing new. Many ladies of the late Victorian era had a naughty little secret under their clothes.

During the 1890s, it became fashionable for trendy Parisian and English women to pierce their nipples. They wore small gold rings on the nipples during the day, known as bosom rings. At night, they might put on more ornate rings for their spouses. Basically, any earring they had could be hung from the nipples. Some even wore strings of pearls attached from one breast to the other. Reportedly, these women liked the way it felt when the nipple rings rubbed against their clothing, and believed that the rings could help make their breasts larger and firmer.

When did women wear "stickers" on their faces?

During the late 1600s, fashionable European ladies might wear little patches on their faces to hide blemishes. The fad evolved into a fashion statement, with women wearing geometrically shaped patches as an adornment. A code of meaning developed, based on where the little stars, moons, or other shapes were placed on the face or bosom. Wearing one below the lip implied that the woman was flirtatious, at the corner of the eye meant passion, by the mouth represented a kiss, and on the cheek denoted a fine lady. Some women covered all the bases and wore a dozen or more at once.

What did the use of hand fans have to do with sex?

While the wearing of facial patches could send signals to others, a lady's hand fan could communicate even more direct sexual signals. At the height of the fan's popularity in the eighteenth century, the way a woman held one could give nonverbal cues to her lover. Holding the fan against the lips meant she wanted a kiss. A wide open fan requested that he be passionate. A slightly open fan would indicate the hour at which they were to meet, according to the number of struts exposed. Numerous other cues were used as well.

So prevalent were these ornate fans that they were banned from many churches. Ladies then adopted very plain, no-frills fans for Sunday worship.

What did Brigham Young have against buttons?

In olden days, some people had a thing against buttons. These prudes felt buttons were immoral because they made it too easy to get out of clothing. When the buttons on men's pants moved from the side to the front, Brigham Young branded them "fornication pants." Happily for him, he didn't live to see the age of the zipper and Velcro.

CHAPTER SEVEN

The Business of Sex

Are sex sites the hottest things on the Internet?

Even after 2001's dot-com meltdown, sex is still the Internet's biggest success story. According to the Online Computer Library Center, there were 74,000 adult Web sites in 2001. That is about two percent of all Web sites. They bring in more than one billion dollars a year. Companies like Cyberotica and Sex.com bring in several million dollars a month. However, online porn is not the cash cow some people once thought it to be.

A commercial Web site can cost from $150 a month to well over $5,000 a month to operate. The Web site owner is charged a fee for the commercial account, as well as transfer fees based on the amount of material accessed from the site. Ninety-five percent of adult-oriented Web sites are very small, generating less than $1,000 per month. There are also loads of eager amateurs posting porn for free, hurting the poor, hardworking, for-profit porn mongers.

Playboy.com is rumored to have lost fifty million dollars in two years. Down but not out, Playboy has been buying up smaller sites and is working on a mobile-phone picture service—Mobile Playmate of the Month. It's success depends on how many users upgrade to new 3G phones and video-enabled terminals.

What's the best Internet porn site guide?

Tired of wasting your time surfing the countless adult Web sites out there to find the ones that really interest you? Check out Jane's

Sex Guide at www.janesguide.com. Their motto is "We waste our time so you don't have to!"

On the Web since 1997, Jane's is kind of like a consumer's report service for porn. They review all kinds of sites, everything from "highbrow erotica and fine art nude photography to xxx hardcore with no redeeming value." You can find amateur sites with real "girl-next-door" photos, vintage pin-ups, and glamour nudes. Jane's will also tell you how much the sites cost and what kind of payments are required.

What is "Naked News"?

If you want totally no-frills news, check out www.nakednews. com. It is an actual, serious newscast, like many others, except the anchors remove their clothing as they read the stories. The on-air talent comes in all shapes, sizes, and genders. They get their news from the wire services, just like other newscasts; the only difference is they disrobe. If you close your eyes and listen to the program, you can't tell it from any ordinary newscast.

The Toronto-based *Naked News* started in 1999, as a single webcast with female anchors. Public interest was piqued by a nod from the *Howard Stern Show* in October 2000. There are now two webcasts; one female and one male. On Friday nights a weekly edition is broadcast on the world's biggest pay-per-view network, iN Demand. The webcasts claim about six million hits per month, as compared to CNN.com, which gets about nine million. *Naked News* is one of the top five shows on iN Demand.

Who is the most downloaded female on the Internet?

There seems to be a bit of animosity between Cindy Margolis and Danni Ashe because of this question. Each claim to be the most downloaded and ogled woman on the Internet. The Guinness Book of World Records initially recognized Margolis as the "Most Downloaded Woman," but gave the title to Ashe in 2000, after they changed the way they calculated downloads. Both gals have impressive numbers. Ashe had 240 million downloads in 1999. While Guinness still considers Ashe the champ, *Yahoo! Magazine* says Margolis is. Their feud is kind of silly because they appeal to different audiences. Ashe's site is more like porn, while Margolis appeals to the PG crowd.

Ashe *is* a porn star, who only does girl/girl scenes on camera. She got her start as a stripper, but found her real calling on the Internet. With an $8,000 investment in computer equipment, she launched her multimillion-dollar Internet business in 1995. Her natural 32FF-23-35 figure is more than enough to draw millions of surfers to her big-chested Web site.

According to Ashe, she is twice as popular as Martha Stewart, three times more popular than Britney Spears and Oprah Winfrey, and fifteen times more popular than Margolis. She says she is so popular that her site uses more bandwidth on a daily basis than all of Central America. Whatever the facts, there's a lot of people looking at her boobs.

What is VoyeurDorm.com?

In case you haven't seen it, VoyeurDorm.com is a site that allows the subscriber to watch the daily goings-on in a Tampa, Florida girl's dorm house. The fifty-five continuously webcasting cameras capture everything the dozen or so girls do, including changing, bathing, and fooling around (penetration and drugs are the only taboos). About 80,000 people pay $34.95 a month to watch. Forty percent of subscribers pay an additional $16.00 a month to chat with the girls. They even hold occasional member parties where the viewers can meet the ladies in person. Some men have become so obsessed with this world of voyeurism that security guards are posted on the dorm's premises twenty-four hours a day.

What do the girls receive in return for baring their lives to thousands of viewers, besides the thrill of being an exhibitionist? They get $400 to $600 a week, plus they are spoiled with many free activities in the house, such as karate and guitar lessons and personal trainers. Not to mention, they receive a great deal of "exposure."

How can you set up your own porn Web site?

Bored with your conventional and unprofitable sex life? Why not set up your own for-profit porn site? One easy way to get your voyeur site up and running is to check out ifriends.com. If you supply your own webcam, the site will provide the software and you split the profits on any pay-per-views or private sessions. But be advised that the Internet porn market is saturated and it takes a lot of viewers to turn a profit. If you need legal advice about this sort of thing, visit the Adult Webmaster Resource Center. Also, check out YNOTmasters. This is a full-service Web site, providing all the resources an adult webmaster needs to start-up and grow an adult-oriented Internet business.

What does Thomas Edison have to do with the peep show?

Photographs of nude women are about as old as the art of photography itself, first appearing in the early 1850s. For a nickel, men could go behind a curtain and look at nude pictures of women. In 1891, Thomas Edison invented the "Kinetoscope," a cabinet that could show a short film to one spectator at a time, but he saw no immediate practical application for his new creation. That was to change in 1894 when he began to manufacture the first peep show machines. The first "Kinetoscope parlor" opened in New York that same year.

In the 1960s, Reuben Struman, a Cleveland businessman, came up with the idea of enclosing coin-operated projectors in small booths, where men could watch a little porn in total privacy. He began by placing peep show booths in his adult bookstores and leased the booths to other porn merchants. Later, he started a company that built the booths and maintained them. They were such a hit that some credit the success of the peep show with the subsequent popularity of the adult film industry.

What are stag movies?

The term "stag" refers to any male animal and comes from the twelfth century Old English word for a "drake," or male duck, *stagge.* The word was later used for a male red deer. By the mid-1800s, the term "stag" became associated with the human male, and male-only parties were called "stag parties." Early stag parties featured men sitting around drinking and looking at grainy photographs of women in various states of undress. Soon after Edison invented moving pictures in the 1890s, these somewhat tame "stag movies" became the main feature of such parties. These films gave way to the raunchier "stag shorts" of the 1930s.

In the 1940s, the first "adult movies" were introduced. They could only be seen in peep shows. By the 1950s, they became known as "blue movies," and could be ordered by mail. They were quite popular at bachelor parties and stag parties. Their quality was low, and their content base.

When did Hollywood begin to censor itself?

During the era of silent movies, the sight of a bare bosom on the silver screen was quite common. There weren't a lot of controls on movie content before the early 1920s but there was a growing public movement to impose governmental guidelines. To avoid such a scenario, the Hollywood studios decided it would be better to censor themselves. In 1930, the Motion Picture Producers and Distributors of America set up the Motion Picture Production Code (also known as the Hays Code) to achieve this end. As their head, they chose Will H. Hays, a member of President Harding's cabinet and a church elder.

Hays established a list of things movies should avoid, such as adultery, scenes that were too passionate, and things that could offend an audience's sensibilities, like rape or seduction used in a comedic context. No-nos also included single beds for married couples, toilets in bathrooms, and any mention of where babies come from. The portrayal of strong marriages and families were encouraged. Savvy directors found ways around the dos and don'ts, as they did on television shows (until just recently). The creative use of innuendo and a wink and a nod gave the viewer the gist of what was supposed to be going on.

These measures, however, were not enough to impress the Catholic Church, which felt Hollywood was still corrupting America. The Catholic Legion of Decency was formed in 1933 to pressure Hollywood to adopt its strict standards. Owing to the fact that the Legion had some ten million members willing to boycott any film that wasn't up to snuff, moviemakers usually caved in to its demands. The Hays Code was put into stricter effect on July 1, 1934, when Joseph I. Breen was appointed director of code administration. Following this, taking the Lord's name in vain and excessive kissing were also prohibited. Screen kisses were actually timed and weren't allowed to last more than one and a half seconds. Bedroom scenes were dicey at best. Even milking a cow was taboo!

Films were rated A, B, or C, with A being virtuous and C being sinful. The legion maintained this leverage over Hollywood until 1956, when Tennessee Williams' *Baby Doll* was released. The legion was against the movie but it was too popular for their boycott attempts to work. From then on, the legion's influence began to wane. Movies the legion thought were indecent, actually experienced increased attendance. By 1965, fully bare breasts reappeared on the screen in the movie *The Pawnbroker*.

Who decides how much skin an actress will show in a movie?

Just like any other part of a movie deal, who shows what is carefully negotiated. Many stars have clauses in their contracts, specifying how much skin they will reveal, down to the inch. Many big names don't show much. Julia Roberts, for example, is quoted as saying, "When you act with your clothes on, it's a performance. When you act with your clothes off, it's a documentary. I don't do documentaries."

Actors don't just hide behind a contract. Movie sets provide flesh-colored socks for the men and patches for the women, if they are feeling modest. Some actresses put black tape on their breasts to be sure the cameramen don't film where they aren't supposed to. For the really prudish star, there is the body double. The stars are allowed to look over the nude bodies of their doubles, to make sure they approve of the assets of the person representing them on screen.

In what movies can you see your favorite TV stars nude?

There isn't really much nudity on American broadcast television, although some of us may wish there were. Who amongst us hasn't once wondered what our favorite TV stars look like in the altogether? (C'mon now!) The following list will tell you what movies to rent if you want to satisfy your dirty little curiosity.

Actress

- Candice Bergen (*Murphy Brown*)
  Soldier Blue (1970)
- Courteney Cox Arquette (*Friends*)
  Blue Desert (1990)
- Jamie Lee Curtis (*Anything But Love*)
  Trading Places (1983)
  Grandview U.S.A. (1983)
  Love Letters (1984)
  Tailor of Panama (2001)
- Tyne Daly (*Cagney & Lacey*)
  The Adulteress (1973)
- Dana Delaney (*China Beach*)
  Light Sleeper (1992)
- Morgan Fairchild (*Falcon Crest*)
  The Seduction (1982)
- Teri Garr (*Good & Evil*)
  One From the Heart (1982)
- Goldie Hawn (*Rowan And Martin's Laugh-In*)
  Criss-Cross (1992)

- Marilu Henner (*Taxi* and *Evening Shade*)
  The Man Who Loved Women (1983)
- Helen Hunt (*Mad About You*)
  The Waterdance (1991)
- Carol Kane (*Taxi*)
  The Last Detail (1973)
- Kristy McNichol (*Empty Nest*)
  Two Moon Junction (1988)
- Tanya Roberts (*Charlie's Angels*)
  Sheena (1984)
  Almost Pregnant (1992)
  Sin of Desire (1992)
- Tracy Scoggins (*Dynasty* and *Lois & Clark: The New Adventures of Superman*)
  The Gumshoe Kid (1990)
  Play Murder For Me (1991)
  Ultimate Desires (1991)
- Jane Seymour (*Dr. Quinn, Medicine Woman*)
  The Tunnel (1987; Spanish)
- Suzanne Somers (*Three's Company*)
  Magnum Force (1973)
- Sally Struthers (*All in the Family*)
  Five Easy Pieces (1970)

Actor

- Jason Alexander (*Seinfeld*)
  The Burning (1981)
- Corbin Bernsen (*L.A. Law*)
  Major League (1989)

- Bruce Boxleitner (*Scarecrow and Mrs. King*)
  Double Jeopardy (1992)
- Pierce Brosnan (*Remington Steele*)
  Live Wire (1992)
- David Carradine (*Kung Fu*)
  The Moderns (1988)
- Jeff Conaway (*Taxi*)
  Almost Pregnant (1992)
- Robert Culp (*I Spy* and *The Greatest American Hero*)
  A Name For Evil (1973)
- Peter Falk (*Columbo*)
  In the Spirit (1990)
- Harry Hamlin (*L.A. Law*)
  Laguna Heat (1987)
- Mark Harmon (*St. Elsewhere* and *Reasonable Doubts*)
  The Fourth Story (1990)
- David Hasselhoff (*Knight Rider* and *Baywatch*)
  Revenge of the Cheerleaders (1976)
- Hal Holbrook (*Evening Shade*)
  The Girl From Petrovka (1974)
- Don Johnson (*Miami Vice*)
  The Harrad Experiment (1973)
  The Hot Spot (1990)
- Ed Marinaro (*Hill Street Blues* and *Sisters*)
  Dead Alm (1987)
- Rob Morrow (*Northern Exposure*)
  Private Resort (1985)
- Edward James Olmos (*Miami Vice*)
  Wolfen (1981)

- Jameson Parker (*Simon & Simon*)
  The Bell Jar (1979)
- Burt Reynolds (*Evening Shade*)
  The Man Who Loved Women (1983)
- Tom Selleck (*Magnum P.I.*)
  Lassiter (1984)
- Tom Skerritt (*Picket Fences*)
  Opposing Force (1986)
  Poison Ivy (1992)
- Robin Williams (*Mork & Mindy*)
  The Fisher King (1991)

These stars appear in various states of undress in the films mentioned. For a complete listing of the stars and the movies in which they bared it, check out Craig Hosoda's wonderful reference book, *The Bare Facts Video Guide*. To check out naked celebs online, try MrSkin.com.

What is the best-selling adult video ever?

The woman who "stars" in the best-selling adult video also starred in the world's most watched television show. Yes, it's Pamela Anderson of *Baywatch* fame.

Pamela Denise Anderson was born in British Columbia, Canada on July, 1, 1967. She became a star when she, and her two silicone-filled boobs, appeared in *Playboy* in 1991. The 5'7", 107-pound blonde bombshell won Playmate of the Year. That lead to her role as C. J. Parker on the enormously popular show *Baywatch*.

One bit of scandal, aside from her stormy relationship with ex-husband Tommy Lee, was the appearance of a stolen sex video of her and Lee. Dubbed the "honeymoon" video, it is a home-made tape shot by the couple, featuring oral sex and intercourse on a boat, in a car, and around the house. Taped for private viewing only, the video was reportedly stolen by a contractor working on the Lee Malibu house in 1995.

Penthouse magazine published stills from the tape in June 1996 and a downloadable Internet version was made available a year later by Internet Entertainment Group (IEG) on their X-rated ClubLove Web site. The Lees filed numerous lawsuits to prevent the tape's release, all in vain. IEG also sold a home-video version for $15 that quickly became the best-selling adult film of all time. In December 2002 a federal judge finally ruled in Pamela and Tommy's favor, saying that IEG owes them $1.5 million in profits made from their tape. They will probably have a hard time collecting, however, since IEG is being dogged by numerous other creditors and founder Seth Warshavsky is said to have left the country.

Are there more adult bookstores or McDonald's restaurants in the U.S.?

According to L. M. Boyd, adult bookstores outnumber McDonald's restaurants by a three-to-one margin. (Apparently, we have a bigger taste for porn than we do for Big Macs.) There are also about 2,500 strip clubs in the United States. A well-managed club can make up to five million dollars a year.

How much is the porn industry worth?

It's hard to put an exact number on such a diverse industry. One has to take into account porn magazines, books, movies, clubs, Internet sites, cable programming, etc. It is estimated, however, that the porn biz grosses more money than all the Hollywood movies and rock and country recordings combined. The trade journal *Adult Video News* put the amount of money spent in 1999 at $10 billion. Sales and rentals of adult videos topped $4 billion in 2001. Motel chains also make a lot of money from porn movies. People spend hundreds of millions to watch this stuff in the privacy of their rooms, for which the motels get a twenty percent cut.

How much does it cost to shoot a porn movie?

Nothing is cheesier or sleazier than a porn movie. This is because they are made in a hurry at rock-bottom prices. Only a few take more than a day to make. The average porn movie costs only about $12,000 to shoot. If it makes $35,000, it's considered a hit. One notable exception is the 1972 porn classic *Deep Throat*, which was made for $22,000 and grossed over $100 million. Its 1:4,546 budget-to-box-office ratio is perhaps the best of any movie ever made. The biggest budget ever for an X-rated film was $17 million for the 1980 Bob Guccione production, *Caligula*.

How much do porn stars earn?

The adult entertainment business is a huge industry, but the stars don't reap much of the profits. Female performers can average between $300 and $1,500 per scene, while the men make $200 to $450. The real moneymaker for the girls is performing at strip clubs, where big-name talent can take in $25,000 a week. This explains why so many porn stars have breast augmentation, since bigger boobs garner bigger tips.

The average working life of an adult film star is about three years, during which an eager beaver can act in up to 300 features. The porn business, centered in Southern California, cranks out about 150 films a week. That's even too much for the most avid hardcore porn aficionado to keep up with.

How do male porn stars perform so reliably?

There have been rumors for years that male porn stars had females known as "fluffers" on the movie set to give them the stimulation they needed to keep it up for the length of time required to complete the scenes being shot. This is basically a myth. The reality is, fluffers are used for gang bangs. In the old days, the men simply used their hand or had the female performer help them out. Producers had to depend on a small stable of actors who possessed the required stamina. Today, however, many rely on Viagra, although many are loathe to admit it.

Do porn stars fake orgasms on screen?

Apparently many of the females actually have on-screen orgasms. The men almost always fake it. The close-ups of a man's face while pretending to come is called a "FIP," or fake internal orgasm. The actual ejaculation, or "money shot," is filmed separately, and is also known as a "pop shot," usually when the man comes on the woman's face. "Cock-ins" are often employed. These are like penis doubles that step in for the male stars for the "monster shot," or close-ups of the erections. Never mind that they may look nothing like the stars unit. Continuity isn't important in porn.

Which porn stars have done the most films/videos?

The champ is the late John C. Holmes. Born John Curtis Estes in 1944, he was a bible student for eleven years in Pataskala, Ohio. To escape his abusive stepfather, John dropped out of high school and joined the Army. After his service, he went to Southern California, where he put his twelve-inch member to work in the porn business. During the late 1960s and early 1970s, he performed in "loads" of adult films. He eventually became a hustler (male prostitute) and a drug addict. Holmes was implicated in the notorious "Laurel Canyon" murders, when his drug-dealer friend Bill Deverell and three others were tortured and killed. He was allegedly present at the murder scene but refused to say anything to authorities. Holmes kept his silence and was acquitted of any wrongdoing in 1981.

All of his fast living later caught up with him when he was diagnosed with AIDS. He died in 1988 at the age of forty-three. He claimed to have had sex with over 10,000 women and he appeared in 2,274 adult films. The Hollywood movie *Boogie Nights* was loosely based on his exploits, although it is said his real life was much wilder than the film.

How did Ron Jeremy get into porn?

The king of porn, Ron Jeremy, has appeared in more than 1,600 adult movies and has been with more than 4,000 women on-screen. He has also directed 250 porn films.

Born Ron Hyatt on March 12, 1953 in Queens, New York, he was raised by a "nice" Jewish family. Jeremy earned a master's degree in education from Queens College and taught high school special education while pursuing a career in acting. His big break came when his girlfriend sent his picture in to *Playgirl* magazine for inclusion in their "Boy Next Door" section. His physical attributes interested the magazine's editors and adult filmmakers alike.

He was cast in his first movie in 1979, *Tigresses . . . And Other Maneaters*. His first on-screen partner was Samantha Fox. From then on, there would always be a lot of work in the business for a well-hung guy who could self-fellate on camera. His parents were supportive of his new profession, though they didn't want him to use the family name.

Ron now directs adult movies and has been a consultant on some Hollywood movies, such as *Boogie Nights* and *9 1/2 Weeks*.

What man had sex with 55 women in one day?

Has to be a porn star, right? You got it. Jon Dough had to have sex with 101 women for the film *The World's Luckiest Man* (Vivid, 1997). Dough cruised through the first day of filming, doing various acts with fifty-five women, and coming about five or six times. He took two weeks to recuperate from this marathon, before polishing off the other forty-six.

Why don't all porn stars wear condoms?

Many of porn's larger production companies, like Vivid and VCA, require all male performers to wear them. Most male stars wouldn't wear them if they had their druthers. This is because the ones who don't wear condoms get paid more and will be offered more roles. Monthly HIV testing is done, and since there aren't many members of the porn fraternity, they feel pretty safe. The testing, however, doesn't protect them from the dangers of other sexually transmitted diseases.

Who holds the world's "gang bang" record?

I'll bet you didn't even know there was such a record. Well, believe it or not, some women really do compete for such a title. On February 10th, 2002, Polish porn star Klaudia Figura managed to have sex with 646 men during a one-day session. She broke the record of 620, held by American porn star Houston since 1999. The record was broken during the First Annual World Gangbang Championship, Part III International Adult Only Festival and Fair Eroticon 2002 in Warsaw, Poland.

Klaudia went up against two other competitors: Mayara from Brazil and Claudia Brown from the United Kingdom. The regulations mandated that each sexual contact had to last between thirty and sixty seconds. Judges closely monitored the proceedings. Claire Brown started out strong, leading for the first hour, but eventually the home-field advantage enabled Klaudia to go for the gusto and pull out the win.

Do any women produce porn movies?

One rap on porn movies from feminists is that they exploit women and treat them as objects. The business is thought to be run by men for a male audience. There are, however, several female adult-movie producers. They crank out the same stuff as their male counterparts, not necessarily any more sensitive to women's feelings or needs. Whether a porn movie is directed by a guy or a woman, they are similar in that the first sex act occurs within about five minutes and they have an average of about seven sex scenes. Female-directed films *generally* feature more woman-on-top scenes, heavy breathing, and penis holding. Male directors like to show erect nipples and guys coming on a girl's face. All in all, both male and female performers seem to be exploited and degraded, regardless of who is directing.

What is obscene pornography?

Most of us can't really define what obscenity is, but know it when we see it. It's all relative. One man's obscenity is another man's art. Technically, pornography is not illegal. Sexually explicit material that is judged in violation of the penal code is deemed obscene and is considered hardcore pornography. Each case is different and courts have yet to decide what is actually legally obscene.

The United States Supreme Court tackled the obscenity issue in the 1957 case *Roth v. United States*. Generally speaking, material is considered obscene to the average person if it is contrary to the contemporary standards of the community, has a predominant appeal to a prurient interest in sex, and has no social, artistic, literary, or scientific value. Good luck in applying those nebulous standards in today's world!

One of the only scientific studies of American pornography usage was conducted in 1970 by the United States Commission on Obscenity. They found that eighty-four percent of men and sixty-nine percent of women had used porn at some time.

How did Playboy get started?

America's foremost playboy, Hugh Hefner, was born in Chicago in 1926. Hugh had a high IQ (152) but was more interested in doodling than getting straight As. He joined the army, where he drew cartoons for army newspapers. After he left the service in 1946, he took art classes at the Chicago Art Institute and enrolled in the University of Illinois, Champaign/Urbana. At U of I, Hugh edited the campus humor magazine *Shaft*, where he introduced a new feature, "Coed of the Month." After college, he worked as a promotional copywriter for *Esquire* magazine in Chicago. When they moved to New York, Hugh stayed behind to start his own publication.

Hugh Hefner started the most famous men's magazine in 1953 with a $500 loan on his apartment furniture. His first issue was produced on his kitchen table. About all he had going for him were the first nude pictures of Marilyn Monroe and the balls to publish them. He was so uncertain about the magazine's future that he didn't even print a date on the first issue. He sold 50,000 copies at fifty cents each, which brought in enough money to do a second issue.

The famous bunny logo appeared on issue number two, and has been on every copy since. The original bunny was a cartoon who wore a tuxedo. Hefner picked the bunny because it had a "humorous sexual connotation," and the tux added sophistication. Hef's biggest problem was the United States Post Office. They tried to stop him from mailing out *Playboy*, early on, but Hefner took them to court and won.

Who has the world's largest collection of porn?

No, it's not Hugh Hefner, although Hef's library of nude photos is prodigious, at nine million. The Institute of Advanced Study of Human Sexuality in San Francisco, a fully accredited graduate school, has a whopping 80,000 erotic books and 150,000 erotic films in its archives. They also have countless posters, playing cards, and other sundry items.

The institute had its origins in 1962, when the United Methodist Church, in cooperation with other Protestant churches, set out to study sexuality in early adulthood. They established study projects in four cities. Methodist minister Reverend Ted McIlvenna headed up the San Francisco group. Today, he is the Institute's president and oversees the massive erotica collection. He has been trying for years to give the collection away, but no one seems to want it.

The Kinsey Institute, in Bloomington, Indiana, comes in second with a collection of 12,000 books, 48,000 photos dating back to the 1870s, 6,000 films, 7,000 videos, and thousands of pieces of erotic art from all over the world, some dating back two thousand years.

What were Tijuana Bibles?

Unless you grew up before the days of men's adult magazines, you probably have never heard of, much less seen, a Tijuana Bible.

They were underground pornographic cartoon books illegally published from the 1930s to the 1950s. Typically eight stapled comic-strip frames, they featured caricatures of characters and celebrities of the time engaged in every sort of sex act imaginable. Those lampooned included Aunt Jemima, Barney Google, Ingrid Bergman, Betty Boop, Al Capone, John Dillinger, Chiang Kai-shek, Gandhi, Lou Gehrig, Rita Hayworth, Benito Mussolini, Joseph Stalin, Popeye, and assorted Disney characters.

Tijuana Bibles were of varying quality—some nothing more than amateurish graffiti, others quite well done. They were sold in barbershops and passed around schoolyards. All male characters had enormous erections and were drawn to look rather goofy. The women were quite fetching and they were all pictured doing something quite filthy while saying humorous dirty dialogue.

There is an active group of people who collect the 700 Tijuana Bibles that survive today. While they were sexist and racist, no group was off-limits. They disparaged everyone equally.

How much do nude models make?

Being an artist's model frequently requires posing nude, but it has nothing to do with porn, and they are paid nothing like naked performers. The average salary for a nude model is between $9.50 and $12 an hour, and they don't get tips for posing especially well. That's hardly enough to live on in many areas. The work is not as easy as it sounds. Models must hold a pose for twenty minutes at a time, during classes that can last from three to six hours.

Nude modeling is a serious profession and they actually have a guild fighting for their rights. One thing the guild wants is a minimum wage of $15 an hour. Another demand is a better work environment. The main venues for the models, both male and female, are art schools, and many of these have less than ideal working conditions. The guild would like to see all schools have private changing rooms (other than the public restroom), heaters (models can get quite chilly during winter term), clean floors, drapes to sit or stand on, and firm rubber mats to better cushion the feet and ankles.

How much do lingerie models make?

It all depends on what your name is. The top names can make up to $40,000 for a big-time runway show, like the Victoria's Secret television special. The top models will also make about $10,000 a day for a Victoria's Secret catalog shoot that may last between one and five days.

What is "Shunga"?

Shunga is a Japanese word that literally translated means "image of spring." In common usage, however, it refers to Japanese erotic paintings of the sixteenth, seventeenth, and eighteenth centuries. They were done by reputable painters of the Ukiyo-e (floating world) period. At the time it was produced, Shunga art was looked down upon and most artists did not sign their work. Shunga was always tastefully done, but depicted explicit sexual acts and human anatomy in full detail. Businessmen used to hang this erotic artwork in halls and charge the public to view it. This is probably one of the earliest forms of the modern pornography industry. Little "pillow books" of Shunga art were used by affluent parents to teach their children about foreplay and sexual technique.

Is bathroom graffiti a modern phenomenon?

Not exactly. Bathroom graffiti is probably as old as is the bathroom itself. Archeologists were surprised to find sexually explicit writings on the walls of excavated Pompeian bathrooms. Buried by the volcanic eruption of Mt. Vesuvius in A.D. 79, were inscriptions such as "Si qui futuere volet Atticen quaerat a XVI" ("If you want to fuck, see Attica No. 16") and "Hic ego puellas multas futui" ("Here I fucked many girls").

What is "queefing"?

Have you ever queefed, ladies? You may have another name for queefs—"pussy farts." Queefs are the result of air escaping from the vagina. A woman is most likely to experience a pussy fart when having intercourse doggy style, as the male thrusting in that position can push air into the vagina that will be expelled when she sits up. A woman can also draw air into her vagina by lying on her back with legs up and sucking in her stomach muscles, while pulling the legs quickly down, or some other such maneuver. You can do your own tests if you wish. Most pussy farts are accidental, but one woman has a unique ability to summon them up on command. She goes by the name "Amber the Lesbian Queefer."

Amber gained notoriety by making it to the finals of the "Miss Howard Stern" contest. (She lost by one vote to "The World's Dumbest Stripper.") Her talent is the ability to queef musical tunes. She has been doing it since she was a teen, and can now queef out such diverse melodies as "The Blue Danube" and "We Will Rock You." Amber can also play the flute with her labia. Does the New York Philharmonic know about this? No, but Mojo Home Video does. They hired her to do a porn video that will highlight her musical vagina.

What is "Puppetry of the Penis"?

There are a couple of guys from Australia who stretch, bend, twist, tie, and otherwise contort their penises onstage to resemble real-life things. David Friend and Simon Morley appear onstage, dressed only in capes, and perform their unique talents in a show called *Puppetry of the Penis*. Subtitled, "The Ancient Art of Genital Origami," their act has been performed throughout the United Kingdom, Australia, and America—in New York, Los Angeles, and San Francisco.

CHAPTER EIGHT

The World's Oldest Profession

When was prostitution sacred?

The first organized "brothels" were actually found in temples. The original Hebrew word for prostitute, *k'deshah*, meant "sacred or holy." The temple whores were called priestesses, and the money they made was used to run the temple. Apart from funding religion, the Romans accepted prostitution because it was seen as a way to keep married women from being seduced and destroying the family structure.

The rise of Christianity helped end this custom, but not entirely. The Catholic Church tolerated prostitution as a "necessary evil." Thomas Aquinas equated it with a sewer pipe in a palace; without it, the palace would be filled with sewage. Martin Luther, however, wanted prostitution outlawed after the Protestant Reformation.

In some Hindu sects, barren women become temple prostitutes in hopes of becoming fertile. They are not supposed to derive any pleasure from this sacred religious function.

Who were the first women to wear lipstick?

While no one is sure that they were the first, it is believed that Egyptian prostitutes who specialized in fellatio first wore lipstick to advertise their oral talents.

What culture required all women to be prostitutes, at least once?

No, it wasn't the ancient Romans, although it was an ancient people: the Mesopotamians. The practice was known as "sacred prostitution." According to Greek historian Herodotus, in ancient Mesopotamia, it was the duty of every female to go to the temple and stay there until a man had paid her in silver to act as a prostitute. Only then would she have fulfilled her holy obligation to Ishtar, goddess of fertility and love, and be free to go home. For the pretty girls it didn't take long, but the unattractive ones could spend quite a while waiting to catch a man's eye. The deformed might have to wait three or four years to satisfy their obligation.

Why are prostitutes called "hookers"?

One popular theory dates back to the American Civil War. Working girls moved with the armies in those days, taking up residence in any town where the soldiers were stationed. Prostitution was such big business during the war that there were 450 brothels in and around Washington, D.C. alone. At least one in ten Union soldiers were treated for venereal disease.

Union general Joseph Hooker, a strict disciplinarian, intended to clean things up while his men were stationed near the nation's capitol. Much to the consternation of the troops, Hooker forbade them from visiting the girls and had the brothels closed down. As a slap in the general's face, the men started referring to the prostitutes as "hookers."

Another theory of the word's first usage comes from Europe. In the 1800s, small boats called "hookers" plied the waters between England and the hook of Holland. The local whores worked the docks, waiting to entice the sailors. They were known by the water men as "hookers."

Perhaps the term is a combination of these two stories. There were Dutch prostitutes working in the Washington, D.C. area at the same time that Hooker's men were there. It would make perfect sense for them to adopt the Dutch word into their vocabulary.

Which was the first state to legalize prostitution?

Your first guess might be Nevada. While that state is famed for its whorehouses, Nevada didn't legalize prostitution until 1974. Missouri has the dubious distinction of being the first state to give the green light to a red-light district in 1872. Brothels and hookers in St. Louis were required by law to register with the city and follow strict guidelines for conducting business. Twenty-five years later, at the urging of Alderman Sidney Story, a semi-legal red-light district known as "Storyville" was created by the city of New Orleans.

Are there still prostitutes in Las Vegas?

Las Vegas was formed in 1905, and prostitution was there right from the very start. The red-light district was known as Block 16. Prostitution flourished there until World War II. When U.S. troops were assigned to the Las Vegas area, the army threatened to declare the place off-limits if it didn't clean up its act. The city subsequently revoked the liquor and gambling licenses of several establishments on Block 16 in 1942, and the bordellos went under.

In 1946, Bugsy Siegel opened the Flamingo Hotel and Casino. The hotel building had wings that allowed customers to return to their rooms with hookers without passing security, police, or others who might be offended. Many casinos subsequently adopted this hotel layout and the prostitutes operated with a greater degree of freedom. In the 1970s, prostitutes plied their trade under the guise of "escort services" and business boomed. So many girls were being arrested that the jails couldn't hold them all. In 1979, the police stopped arresting prostitutes and began simply fining them. This opened the floodgates and prostitutes flocked to the city like never before.

A major change transformed Las Vegas in the 1990s. Businessmen realized there was a lot of money to be made from family-oriented entertainment. Several huge hotel/amusement resorts opened up. The smut peddlers, who handed out flyers and color brochures for "escorts" to anyone walking down the street, had to go. The police cracked down on street smut in 1996, and it is now virtually nonexistent. Hookers are now found under "adult entertainment" in the Yellow Pages.

What's a Nevada brothel like?

Prostitution is illegal in all U.S. states, except certain counties in Nevada. Only Nevada cities with populations below 200,000 allow brothels. All told, there are only about thirty cathouses in the whole state, and they are all geared for male customers. It is not illegal to have brothels for women; there just doesn't seem to be enough demand to make them profitable.

The following four questions reflect the present-day brothel customs found in Nevada.

What do you do when you walk into a brothel?

After parking your car, walk up to the door and ring the buzzer. You must be buzzed in. This is to prevent drunks or unwitting tourists with children from stumbling in. Once inside, you will probably be greeted by the shift manager. If you are in a Las Vegas-area brothel, you will be shown a lineup of girls right away, in the parlor area. If you are in the Reno or Carson City areas, you be shown a lineup, or you may sit at the bar and get a drink, or mingle.

If there's a lineup, the girls will quickly introduce themselves to you and the manager will ask if you are ready to pick one, or if you would like to talk to some first. If you can't decide, go to the bar, if they have one, and have a seat. If the house doesn't have a lineup, just have a seat and you will be approached by the girls. They will approach you singly and start a conversation to find out if you want to "party" with them. Once you pick a girl, you can get a tour of the house or go right to her room for negotiations (see next question).

Don't feel pressure to pick a girl if you are uncomfortable. It is common for men to check out several brothels before settling on the right house or girl.

How much do brothels charge?

Each brothel has an established minimum. The fee may range from $60 to $200. The girls, however, are independent contractors and can charge as high as they like. You can probably count on dropping about $400 for an average visit. Different girls in the same house may charge significantly different fees. Usually, the more popular ladies command a higher price.

The "minimum party" is the fee that is charged for the shortest visit, normally around twenty minutes, which probably involves simply a hand job or blow job, not intercourse. Many girls have a menu with increasing fees for the various sex acts to be performed. But remember, you can negotiate any fee. There may be some pricing flexibility, depending on how busy the girl or the house is and how attractive *you* are. The lady may well charge a drunk, unclean, or otherwise undesirable customer more than a nice, clean, polite guy. If she really doesn't like you, she will name a price so high that you will say "forget it."

Price negotiations are normally conducted in the girl's room. The house has an intercom system that management uses to listen in on the price agreed. This is to ensure they get their fifty percent cut of the transaction. Paying the girl extra under the table is illegal; however, you may tip her. Some houses take a cut of the tip as well, so you may want to keep quiet while slipping her a few extra dollars.

What happens after you agree to a price?

Once you pay the girl her money, it's time for your health inspection. While these ladies are not nurses, they have a fair degree of experience with the male anatomy. She will ask you to drop your drawers and will proceed to thoroughly examine your penis. The inspection involves squeezing it to see if anything comes out and looking for sores. If you pass, she will tell you to "get more comfortable" while she arranges the party. This means take off your clothes, at least down to your underwear, and get on the bed. Do not, however, get under the covers! This is considered personal space and is not for you.

When she comes back, she will lay a clean sheet or towel on the bed and proceed to wash your genitals, either at the sink or on the bed with a basin of warm soapy water. They refer to this bowl as the "peter pan." She then may wash herself as well. Then, it's down to business. When your time is up, there will be a knock at the door, or a voice on the intercom telling you it's time to renegotiate. The girl will then either hand you a paper towel, or she may wash you up herself if she really wants a tip.

After you both get dressed, she will walk you back to the parlor area. Now you can either leave, sit at the bar, or negotiate with a girl for another go around.

Do hookers kiss?

The mouth-to-mouth kissing of a working girl is just about taboo. Most of these ladies seem to consider it a "personal act," (as if giving a blow job isn't a personal act) reserved for the one they love. There is also the question of hygiene. Condoms protect the girls from germs during intercourse or oral sex, but kissing involves direct contact of body fluids. Most brothels have a house rule against it.

Where can you find the cheapest hookers?

There are cheap women and then there are *cheap* women. Perhaps the lowest priced prostitutes in the world can be found in Bangladesh (an appropriate name). There is a border town there called Petrapole that is situated on a major truck route. Up to five million truckers a year avail themselves of the local working girls while waiting to cross the border. Some fellows buy sex every time they cross the border. One reason business is so good is the incredibly low prices the girls charge. For a mere ten rupees (about twenty-eight cents) a man can get his rocks off.

Why is the red-light district so named?

Early whorehouses traditionally displayed their girls right out on the street or in large windows in front of their shops. Passersby could easily be lured into these dens of inequity by the scantily clad prostitutes. This blatant form of advertising began to change in medieval China. By the thirteenth century, the Chinese had encouraged their social elite to visit more discreet brothels. The girls were removed from the storefronts and, in their place, red silk-covered bamboo lanterns were hung. The lanterns served as a subtle signal to Chinese gentlemen looking for some female companionship. The color red was chosen, as it was the Chinese color for good fortune.

The red-light district came to America during the California Gold Rush. Chinese brothel owners brought their little red lights along with their Chinese whores, who serviced the multitude of Chinese railroad workers. It wasn't long before other American brothels adopted the red light.

Why isn't prostitution as popular as it used to be?

The world's oldest profession is losing customers. In the old days, a brothel was the place to go to get your rocks off. In our modern world, however, people have many alternatives. Internet and video porn have hurt business, as has the fear of AIDS. But perhaps the most damage has been done by the sexual revolution of the 1960s and 1970s. With all the birth control options available today, men are more likely to find "free" sex with a woman than at any other time in recorded history. That is, if he has enough money for dinner and a movie.

What popular beer has a hooker on its label?

The label of St. Pauli Girl beer has a buxom German beauty serving up six mugs of brew. St. Pauli Girl is named for the St. Pauli neighborhood of Hamburg, Germany, which was historically a red-light district. This leads one to believe that beer may not be the only thing that a St. Pauli girl might serve up.

What are sex surrogates?

It depends on who you ask. Some people consider them to be real therapists, and others call them prostitutes. If they advertise for business, they are probably not legitimate therapists. Those that are referred by psychologists or sex therapists are usually legitimate. Good surrogates have gone through a twelve-week training course that teaches human anatomy, communication, and sexual response.

The idea of sex surrogates took off in the 1970s but has declined in popularity since then. Predictably, sex surrogates are primarily found on the West Coast. They are looked upon as an integral part of the sex treatment team. The course of treatment can run from seven to fourteen weeks or more for older patients, and can cost about $200 for a two-hour session. Good sex surrogates say they don't have sex with a patient right off the bat. Intercourse may not take place until after the surrogate has seen the patient several times, if it occurs at all. The therapist should be involved at all stages and give the go-ahead for intercourse. At this point, the patient is usually deemed to be cured. Surrogates are supposed to emphasize sensuality, not sexuality. Predictably, most clients are men.

In Japan, they have something called "sex volunteers." The Sex Volunteer Corps consists of men who are recruited to provide sex to women in sexless marriages. Corps founder, Kim Myung Jun, says he started this program to help repair the damaged self-esteem of women.

Is phone sex a rip-off?

Phone sex can be hazardous to your wallet. They can really nail you with the long-distance phone charges. Since many phone sex companies operate outside of the United States, there is very little regulation, and they prey on unsuspecting callers.

For example, the international access code is 011, but many phone sex lines have area codes that make it appear that they are domestically-based outfits. A lot of them are in the Caribbean, with phone numbers starting with 809, or in Canada, with numbers beginning with 604. Many customers do not realize that these are international calls and will cost them big-time. The phone sex people get kickbacks from the phone companies to make the whole little scheme profitable for both of them.

Phone sex companies charge between $1.99 to $4.99 per minute, with the average call costing between $25 and $100. Meanwhile, the operators who work for these sex merchants only make about $12 per hour.

Is a geisha a prostitute?

The Japanese culture of the past put little importance on the idea of romantic love. Most marriages were arranged. Husbands and wives often did not love one another. A wife was a servant and a mother. Men sought conversation and sexual gratification outside the home. The Japanese man had two choices: a prostitute (*yoshiwara*) for sex, or a geisha for conversation and female companionship. While a man could have a sexual relationship with a geisha, it was very expensive and was the equivalent of having a mistress. Any male children born to a geisha belonged to the father and were raised in his home by his wife. Female children were the responsibility of the geisha.

There are not that many geisha anymore. These Japanese female entertainers were set apart from common prostitutes by their learning and culture. Beginning at the age of twelve, they were educated in the arts. For the next six years the geisha was trained in traditional music and dance, social etiquette, the precise rituals of the tea and flower-arranging ceremonies, and the art of conversation.

Geisha were bought entertainers and had a perfect right to refuse sex; most often did. However, geisha needed to be provided for. As such, geisha were like stay-at-home wives who needed steady employers: husbands. The geisha needed to attract a man who was wealthy enough to provide for her needs. She had no more interest in love and marriage than did the man, who was usually already married anyway. She was more a kept woman than a prostitute.

Geisha used to undergo a rite of passage known as *mizuage*, which was a compulsory deflowering. Most geisha underwent this rite at age fourteen. The deflowering was done by a wealthy patron, who would agree to look after the young girl. The patrons paid big money for the honor of deflowering the young virgin and this was a very important business transaction in the girl's life. As vulgar as we may view this practice today, it must be viewed in the context of the times. One way or the other, a young Japanese girl was going to be deflowered by someone she barely knew or cared about. Either she would lose her virginity to her husband in an arranged marriage or she would lose it through *mizuage*.

Sex in Japan was more casual before 1958, when an anti-prostitution bill was enacted. The bill didn't effect the geisha directly as they weren't prostitutes, but it increased their competition, as many whores cleaned themselves up and tried to pass themselves off as legitimate geisha.

What famous Vatican structure's construction was funded through prostitution?

The long arm of the Catholic Church even had its hand in the prostitution business during the Middle Ages. Pope Clement II, who sat from 1046 to 1047, issued a papal bull requiring anyone who was ever a prostitute to leave half their property to the Church when they died. Queen Joanna of Naples established one of the first Church-controlled brothels in the papal city of Avignon, which she called an abbaye (abbey). The ladies who resided there were required to attend regular prayer meetings and church services. The most famous Vatican building, St. Peter's Basilica, was partly funded through a Church-imposed tax on prostitution that had been initiated in the Middle Ages. So great were the earnings from the prostitution tax that they greatly exceeded the money raised by the sale of indulgences.

In 1501, Pope Alexander VI even had orgies at the Vatican, one involving some fifty prostitutes, with prizes given out to the participants with the most stamina. Alexander must have enjoyed engaging in sex himself. He is reported to have fathered seven illegitimate children.

CHAPTER NINE

Toys and Techniques

What are our favorite sex acts?

We all have our own individual tastes when it comes to sex. Men and women tend to be a little different in their preferences. A book called *The Book of Sex Lists*, by Albert Gerber, lists a ranking of America's top ten sexual acts.

The top ten sex acts for heterosexual men are as follows:

1. fellatio
2. intercourse in a variety of positions
3. nude encounters with two women
4. fondling a women's breasts
5. anal intercourse with a woman
6. performing cunnilingus while the woman performs fellatio
7. performing mild S&M acts on a woman
8. getting a hand job from a woman
9. performing cunnilingus
10. masturbation

Heterosexual women, on the other hand, had the following sexual preferences:

1. gentle cunnilingus by a man
2. gentle finger stimulation of the clitoris by a man
3. intercourse in the missionary position

4. intercourse in other varying positions
5. receiving cunnilingus while performing fellatio
6. massaging a man all over
7. giving a man a hand job
8. being masturbated by a woman
9. masturbation
10. performing fellatio

How do men and women differ in their fantasies?

We all have sex fantasies, whether we admit it or not. Some are wild, some are tame. However, men and women generally fantasize in different ways.

The typical male sex fantasy is big on visuals and there are usually no emotional strings attached. This is why porn movies are a big hit with men. It makes their testosterone levels rise, among other things.

Women generally fantasize about long-term relationships with a high level of emotional attachment. This is because, evolutionarily speaking, women want mates who will stick around and help raise the young. Some women can have orgasms just from fantasizing. Proof of the female fantasy can be seen in the billion-dollar romance-novel market, which is targeted almost exclusively toward women.

What are "Kegels"?

Kegel exercises are a rhythmic clenching and unclenching of the pubococcygeal (PC) muscle. This is the muscle extending from your pubic bone to your tailbone. The PC muscle encircles the urinary opening, the anus, the perineum, and the vaginal opening. It is the muscle you use to keep from urinating. As people age, the muscle gets weaker and incontinence can follow. The exercises involve contracting the muscles you use to stop the flow of urine and holding the contraction for a few seconds. This is repeated ten times in a row and should be done several times a day.

In 1946, Los Angeles obstetrician/gynecologist Dr. Arnold Kegel developed these exercises to strengthen the PC muscle as a remedy for incontinence and as an alternative to surgery for women. Mothers also can use them to tighten up the vagina after childbirth. However, a sexual benefit to performing Kegels was soon found.

How can you use Kegels in your lovemaking?

Since the PC muscle also encircles the vaginal opening, women who have strengthened it can perform Kegels during intercourse to grip their partner's penis. Known as "pompoir," this technique can enable a woman to bring a man to orgasm simply by moving the muscles of her vagina and pelvis. It takes a long time for a woman to build up her muscles to this point and plenty of practice in manipulating those muscles, but it's said to be well worth the effort.

What is "snowballing"?

Also known as the "ice trick," snowballing was first written about in John Eichenlaub's *The Marriage Art* (1962), and later popularized in the 1977 film, *The Other Side of Midnight*.

This sexual technique involves applying ice to the genitals just before ejaculation to produce a stronger orgasm. Snowballing works so well because the ice triggers the cremaster muscles to contract even tighter than they normally do in response to sexual stimulus, due to the "cold response" (see page 9).

What sexual position is called "the 20"?

Most of you are probably familiar with the more common "69" position, in which the male and female participants lie in opposite directions while administering oral sex to one another, forming a somewhat 69-shaped figure with their bodies. The "20" is a variant of the 69, in which the partners suck on each others toes instead of the genitals. The "20" comes from the number of toes involved (ten plus ten), not the body positions.

What sex game is called "goldfish"?

No, it doesn't have anything to do with an aquarium. This novel way of making love is described in *The Joy of Sex* by Alex Comfort. In it, a naked couple have their hands tied behind their backs and they are placed on a mattress. The participants then must make love like the fish—without hands. Goldfish was a popular bordello game of the nineteenth century, and is also a hit at kinky twenty-first-century parties.

What is axillism?

A more common sexual practice in Europe, where women let their underarm hair grow, axillism is basically a man masturbating in a woman's armpit. With the arm down, a nice tight fit can be achieved around a man's penis as he thrusts in and out. This is a good form of safe sex.

How are bees used in sex?

Although not a common practice, the use of bees in lovemaking is certainly a curious one. Bees can be held against the penis, just below the glans, and encouraged to sting. This will produce itching, and swelling of the member. A string is tied around the base of the penis to prevent the swelling from spreading into the body. Swelling will persist for several days. By day two, a fifty percent increase in circumference is not unusual.

(Please have a brain in your head and do *not* try this. Thank you.)

What is the best wine to serve on your lover's genitals?

That eternal question, red or white? Are you one of those people who enjoy a drink of wine or champagne before sex, or even during sex? Those of you who are somewhat adventurous with sex and drink may have even tried a little of the bubbly on your lover's more sensitive body regions. It may interest you to know that certain wines go better with the genitals than others. At least that is what one book claims.

A book called *Oral Sex Made Easy* (International Sex Institute, 1982) says that while champagne's effervescence may tickle the fancy of the one slurping the libation, "its dry flavor does not combine well with the natural aroma of the woman's vulva." They claim a bubbly sweet wine is a better choice. The book also recommends avoiding wines that have an alcohol content of greater than twelve to fourteen percent, as they can cause a burning sensation down below.

Perhaps the best beverage served over a woman's genitals is orange juice. It is said to reduce the smell of the vulva, which some people may find offensive.

What is an "anal violin"?

Have you ever had a lover who played you like an instrument, figuratively speaking? Possibly. But did you know that there is a sexual device that allows your partner to *literally* play you like a violin? Known as an "anal violin," it is an anal masturbation device of the Orient, consisting of a hard-boiled egg or an ivory or wooden ball, to which a length of catgut string is attached. Can you guess the rest? That's right, the egg or ball is inserted into the anus, and the string is pulled taut and played with a violin bow. The vibrations are said to produce a very stimulating anal sensation. While this technique may be music to the anus, it is almost certainly not music to the ears.

The anal violin was quite popular among the eunuchs of the Ottoman Empire. (Desperate times call for desperate measures.) Modern electric versions are now available for your listening pleasure.

What sex aid is called a "goat's eyelid"?

This rather odd sounding sex aid was one of the oldest forms of the cock ring, a device used to prolong an erection and give a woman pleasure. Originating in the thirteenth century in the Orient, the goat's eyelid really *was* made from the eyelid of a goat. It was introduced to the Mongol emperors from Tibetan lamas.

A goat was killed and the eyelids and eyelashes were put in quicklime to dry, then steamed for at least twelve hours in a bamboo basket. After going through this process several times, they would be fit around the glans penis. Not only did it help maintain an erection, but it also provided a pleasurable sensation in the vagina during intercourse.

There are modern plastic versions available for your pleasure. They are from one-and-a-half to two inches in diameter and are slipped over the erect penis and testicles, which puts pressure on the dorsal vein of the penis and keeps the blood from flowing out. For those of you on a budget, a simple rubber band can also be put around the base of the penis to prolong an erection. Some guys wear them under their clothes to give the illusion of a big unit.

CAUTION: Wearing cock rings that are too tight or for too long a period of time can cause severe damage to the genitals!!

Can a woman have orgasms at the push of a button?

This may sound like some far-out sex gizmo from the futuristic Woody Allen movie *Sleeper*, but a North Carolina pain-relief surgeon has *really* stumbled across an electronic device that can give women multiple orgasms at the touch of a button. Dr. Stuart Meloy of the Piedmont Anaesthesia and Pain Consultants made his surreptitious discovery while performing a routine pain-relief operation on a woman's spine.

The procedure involves implanting electrodes into the spine and sending electrical impulses through them to modify the pain signals passing along the nerves. Patients remain awake throughout the operation to help the surgeons determine the best place to attach the electrodes for maximum pain relief. During one such procedure, the good doctor placed the electrodes in an area that didn't do much for her pain, but gave her great sexual stimulation and orgasms.

Now an electrical generator, the size of a pack of cigarettes, is being developed that can be implanted into the buttocks. The implant's electrodes will be attached to the orgasm stimulation site, and the patient will be supplied with a handheld remote control to trigger an orgasm. While this invention sounds great, Dr. Meloy envisions its use being limited to those patients who suffer from extreme orgasmic dysfunction. Even then, it would be programmed to limit the number of orgasms a patient could have in a given period of time. What that number would be is open to debate. They don't want women sitting around having orgasms all day long at the push of a button. That kind of sexual freedom could change the civilized world as we know it!

What's a Make Your Own Dildo Kit?

Not happy with the shapes and sizes of the dildos available on the market? Try the Make Your Own Dildo Kit. If you are a do-it-yourselfer and enjoy at home projects, you can create a custom-made dildo in the comfort of your own home. Thousands of people already have. The beauty of this kit is that you can make a dildo mold from any willing male model. Then, even if that special someone is away, you will always have his member, or at least a reasonable facsimile, at the ready. The Make Your Own Dildo Kit can be found at Goodvibes.com.

What is a "dolfinger"?

The ever innovative Japanese have come up with a dolphin-shaped sex toy that is worn on the underside of a finger. It is soft and includes a "Technobeat Vibe" to increase your partner's pleasure, or your own.

Another vibrating device popular in Japan is the Puru Puru Cherry. Its design was inspired from suggestions made from female viewers to the operators at the satellite channel Cherry Bomb. The creation has two small, cherry-shaped orbs that vibrate in opposite directions. Unlike other vibrating devices, Puru Puru Cherries shake randomly. The user has no idea when the cherries are going to start moving around. This is supposed to add the thrill of the unexpected. They are small enough to be used outside or inside the body.

For those of you who prefer illuminated toys, there are the Tokyo Night View and Yokahama Bay Bridge, which are phallic-shaped sex toys made of transparent plastic with fiberoptic lights inside. When turned on, they light up to resemble a cityscape after dark.

If you prefer to get even more visual in your sex play, Omochannel.com sells a vibrator that has a miniature video camera inside. Just hook it up to a TV or video for in-depth coverage of the proceedings.

And finally, the high-tech-addicted Japanese have also come up with a long-distance, remote-controlled vibrator: My Wave. Designed to be worn throughout the day, My Wave can be activated via cell phone. This long-distance vibrator can help keep separated lovers in touch in more ways than one.

What are anal inserts?

One type of anal insert are anal plugs. They are shaped like inverted cones or fingers. Men can insert them into the rectum to stimulate the prostate. Women can insert them to fill the rectal cavity so that they will press against the inner vagina, making it smaller and thus resulting in greater pleasure during intercourse.

Another type of anal insert is known as Chinese love beads, or String of Pearls. These are small rubber balls, attached about an inch apart, on a string. They are slowly pulled out of the anus during ejaculation. A similar effect is achieved with a knotted, silken handkerchief. This variation is known as the Briggs-Stratton Effect or Seven Knots to Heaven.

What is a Love Light?

People may take several steps to put their partner in the mood: food, drinks, music, lingerie, candles, and incense. These are all good precursors to lovemaking, but the British electricity supplier,

Powergen PLC, has come up with one more mood enhancer: the Love Light.

What is a power company doing making Love Lights? Powergen set out to research the best kind of lighting for work and relaxation. In their study they found that light, color, and movement, at different intensities and sequences, could cause certain people to become sexually aroused. When tested on couples, red light gave feelings of warmth, coziness, and romance, but not physical desire. Green light produced cold, distant feelings and jealousy. But yellow light did the trick when it came to making couples horny.

Powergen is marketing their six-foot-long, eighteen-inch-wide Love Light in Britain. It can be put in any room and has settings for color, intensity, and speed. While the light's optimum effects can be found by experimenting with the settings, the company warns that it does not work on all people.

What popular sex toy was originally a medical device?

For every great invention there has to be an inventor. In the case of the vibrator, we can thank two people: Englishman Mortimer Glanville and American Dr. George Taylor. Neither of these men had intended to create a sex toy. They viewed their inventions as strictly medicinal.

The women of the Victorian era were a very sexually deprived bunch. Physicians of the time even had a name for this condition, "hysteria," from the Greek for "uterus." At least half of Victorian women were believed to have suffered from hysteria, whose symptoms included, anxiety, irritability, sexual fantasies, and "excessive" vaginal lubrication (in other words, they were horny). The proper ladies of the time sought help from their physicians, who would manually "manipulate" their clitoris until the anxiety was relieved. This was a tiring and time-consuming procedure for the doctors and they were happy when a therapeutic device finally became available. Health spas of the day also catered to these women, with special water-jet "treatments," designed to relieve their sexual tensions.

During the 1860s, Dr. Taylor created a large, cumbersome, coal-fired, steam-driven massaging machine—not at all practical for home use. Twenty years later, Mortimer Glanville came along and improved on Taylor's idea. He used the new technology of battery power to reduce the size of Taylor's contraption. He called his new vibrating massager a "percuteur." Glanville intended it to be used as a male muscle massager and warned against its use on women. Doctors, however, ignored his advice and quickly started using the percuteur to treat hysteria.

What sex aid was sold in the Sears catalog?

Vibrators were used exclusively by doctors up until the turn of the twentieth century. By 1900, there were over a dozen manufacturers, cranking out both battery-powered and plug-in models. The plug-in vibrator quickly became a popular device in the new, electric-age home, along with the electric sewing machine, tea kettle, and toaster. During the 1910s and 1920s, vibrator sales were mainly mail order. The 1918 Sears Roebuck catalog sold them. At $5.95, they were advertised as an aid "every woman appreciates." Once they began to appear in erotic movies, "respectable" magazines shunned them and advertisements disappeared until the 1950s. From this decade on, advertisements in magazines referred to vibrators as "massagers" or "spot reducers," alluding to their supposed use in weight reduction. In the 1960s, they were marketed as "beauty aids."

Then, as now, many massaging devices are sold under the guise of muscle therapy, when they are in fact used for sexual pleasure. The portable one-piece plastic vibrator, shaped like a cigar and battery-powered, was developed by Jon H. Tavel in 1966. Today, it is estimated that two percent of American women own vibrators. (Sounds a bit low.)

What is a "ball stretcher"?

This painful-sounding sex gadget consists of metal rings or leather straps that fasten around the top of the scrotum and force it down. Weights may also be employed. The ball stretcher prevents the cremaster muscles from pulling the testicles close to the body as normally would happen during foreplay and orgasm. The result is that of delayed ejaculation, followed by a prolonged orgasm. Many men achieve the same effect by having their partner pull down on their testicles. This can be somewhat painful but hey, whatever gets your rocks off.

How can you use Altoids to improve your sex life?

While some people may need a breath mint after giving oral sex, certain practitioners of the art prefer to suck on mints beforehand. The mucous membranes, including the genitals, are particularly sensitive to mint oils, which penetrate the skin to give sensations of warmth or cold. One favorite brand of mints used for this purpose is Altoids. They are made from real peppermint oil and are thus stronger than most other mints. If you suck on a couple just before pleasuring your partner, you can give hot or cold tingly feelings to their genitals. By inhaling or blowing close to their genitals, you can produce warming or cooling sensations. This effect works equally well on women and men.

What are ben-wa balls?

Ben-wa balls originated in ancient China. Also known as Burmese balls, they were originally hollow spheres made of metal or ivory, one of which had a large bead of mercury inside. The other ball was empty or had a metal "tongue." The balls were inserted into the vagina and the woman would rock back and forth. The mercury caused the balls to roll around and clack against one another, stimulating the vagina.

Today, the device consists of three balls, one of which is hollow. Mercury, which is poisonous, is not used. Therefore, they don't roll around much and give little pleasure.

A newer version of ben-wa balls are "thunder balls." They are two plastic balls with smaller weighted balls inside, attached by a string, which is used to remove them from the vagina. Thunder balls are bigger than ben-wa balls, so they feel better going in and out. A variation on ben-wa balls are anal beads. They consist of five plastic or rubber balls linked together on a cord. A number of the balls are inserted into the anus and pulled out to stimulate the rectum.

What scuba diving product is used for sex?

There is a product called Slippery Stuff that is probably the best water-based lubricant for the bedroom ever invented. It is a polyethylene oxide originally developed to help scuba divers slip into their wet suits. Slippery Stuff is so slippery that when used for intercourse, a man experiences such little friction on the penis that he may be able to prolong his lovemaking. (Some gel lubricants have numbing properties that can also keep him erect longer.) Another good water-based lubricant is Astroglide.

Do any sexual lubricants kill the AIDS virus?

The medical journal *AIDS Research and Human Retroviruses* published a study in late 2002 stating this to be the case. The research was funded by the National Institutes of Health, the MacArthur Foundation, and the University of Texas. In the study, small amounts of twenty-two different over-the-counter sexual lubricants were mixed with HIV-infected semen. Three of the lubricants were found to reduce HIV replication by more than 99.9 percent. The three lubricants were Astroglide (also sold as Silken Secret), Vagisil, and ViAmor. The names of the lubricating ingredients that kill the virus will be released soon.

No tests have yet been done to see if Astroglide and the others will actually kill HIV during sex, so continue to use a condom. Apart from any HIV-prevention value of these products, lubricants help prevent condom breakage, which is also a plus. The researchers are encouraging the United States and the United

Nations to continue testing to see if these products are effective in real-life situations.

Since these lubricants are widely used and inexpensive, they could easily be used by people in Africa, where AIDS is a major problem and condom use is frowned upon.

What is "tantric sex"?

Tantra is a kind of sexual spiritualism that evolved in the sixth century A.D. among Buddhists and Hindus. It is a path to enlightenment that conforms to the belief that the greatest source of energy in the universe is sexual. Tantric sex is considered sacred and divine. It involves the body, mind, and spirit.

Practitioners seek to find divinity (and the universe) through tantric sex, during which the man remains in the woman for prolonged periods without ejaculating. Masters of the tantric technique can even experience orgasms without ejaculating. This can be achieved through great muscle control and/or applying pressure to the perineum, allowing the man to keep an erection for up to an hour or more. Maintaining eye contact with your partner is also a key to the spiritual enlightenment that tantric practitioners are after. You use your sexual energy to merge in ecstasy with your partner, and through them, with the universe.

The art of prolonging sex in this way is described in the *Kamasutra*, an Indian tantric scripture, written by third-century Hindu ascetic Vatsyayana. The *Kamasutra* is a treatise (sutra) on sex, love, and pleasure (Kama's the Hindu god of love). In it, Vatsyayana explores the myriad ways of having sex. He describes eight stages of oral sex, several kinds of scratching and biting, and thirty positions for intercourse. The curious thing is, being an ascetic, Vatsyayana probably didn't have sex himself.

CHAPTER TEN

A Brief History of Sex

When did women have to pay to be raped?

Rape is a terrible crime, but imagine if the rapist charged a fee. Such was the case with ancient Roman rulers. They told their subjects that they were the living embodiment of the gods on earth. As such, they wielded power over harvests and fertility. The Romans adopted a Sumerian custom and decreed that for a woman to be fertile, she must be deflowered by the ruler on her wedding night. This ritual came to be called "the right of the first night." To add insult to injury, it was required that the bridegroom pay a fee for this service, which the ruler claimed was quite a burden on him. Those who could not pay the fee could not get married. Quite a racket.

As time went on, this reprehensible practice changed. The Roman rulers couldn't personally deflower all the young women in the burgeoning population, so an alternate means of ensuring fertility needed to be found. During public wedding ceremonies, the bride was required to straddle a stone statue of the fertility god, Liber, lowering herself onto this effigy. The phallic-shaped stone was intended to rupture her hymen if it was still intact. This bloody self-deflowering demonstrated to the crowd that she indeed was a virgin and would be fruitful.

The right of the first night was such a popular idea among the powerful that it continued in Europe into feudal times. However, the lord of an estate made no pretext of being godly and the practice had nothing to do with fertility or the harvest. It was simply his right to deflower any girl on his lands who got married. This right is memorably depicted in the movie *Braveheart*.

The right of the first night even came to America. Southern slave owners could invoke "the master's obligation," which some slave owners used in order to claim that it was their duty to have sex with a black bride on her wedding night.

When was Cupid the symbol of pedophilia?

The cute angelic Cupid that adorns Valentine's Day cards today wasn't always as innocent as you may have thought. The little guy was a symbol for pedophile love among the ancient Greeks. His name was Eros, and his likeness was found in gymnasiums where men and boys exercised in the nude. Cupid originally was naked, too. He was the male concept of the perfect homosexual lover. Over time, Eros was depicted as being younger and younger. He grew wings and acquired a bow and arrow.

The Romans knew this cute Eros as "Cupido," or "carnal desire." It was the sexually repressive Victorians who decided to clothe Cupid and make him the innocent childlike image we know today.

What does hanging a horseshoe over a door have to do with sex?

Stone carvings of vaginas in India date back to 35,000 B.C. The ancients believed in the wearing of charms to ward off evil, ensure a good harvest, and promote fertility. They thought that a woman's genitals or "yoni" (sanskrit for womb), the giver of life, had magical powers, and yoni worship was practiced. A woman could break evil spells, cure the sick, or even change the weather just by exposing herself. As such, charms in the shape of the yoni were worn around the neck and hung over the doors of temples. The symbols resembled an oval with an open bottom.

This old custom is still seen today in the tradition of hanging an upside-down horseshoe over doorways for good luck. It also is used by some lesbians as a sign of their proclivities.

Phallic charms were worn by the ancient Romans to ward off the evil eye. They also placed phallic figures in their gardens to ensure a good crop.

What empress demanded all visitors to her court to perform cunnilingus?

During the T'ang Dynasty (700–900 A.D.), there was an empress named Wu Hu who felt superior to men. She believed that a woman performing fellatio on a man gave that man superiority. To give her the upper hand, she compelled all visiting male dignitaries and government officials to her court to kneel before her and lick her clitoris. She would open her robe so that homage could be paid. (It's good to be queen!)

Another odd way of showing respect to a ruler is found in a pre-Christian Irish myth, which says that the Queen of Ulster and all 610 ladies of her court went to meet the hero Cuchalainn topless and lifted their skirts to honor him.

Which ancient rulers had so many wives that they needed sex secretaries?

You know your sex life is complicated when you need special secretaries just to keep track of when you have intercourse and with whom. While this "problem" may be the envy of some men today, it was a strict matter of duty for the ancient Chinese emperors.

These rulers were required to have one queen, three consorts, nine second-rank wives, twenty-seven third-rank wives, and eighty-one concubines. They believed this exact combination of sexual partners fit their "magical numbers." The emperor was on a strict sex schedule and had special "sex secretaries" to work out the order of his performances. The schedule was set so that he had sex with the lower wives in progression up to the queen, who had intercourse with him once a month. It was believed that his "yin" (male sexual power) was strengthened from his intercourse with all the lesser wives. Ironically, all this sex probably had the exact opposite effect on his fertility with the queen.

The emperor was not the only man in China to have several wives. A Chinese marriage often included the bride's sisters and maids. These familiar faces, as well as the husband's secondary wives, helped ease the bride's transition into her new home. Sons often had affairs with their father's secondary wives, as husbands only saw these women at the dinner table or in bed. When a new concubine was introduced into the Chinese household, she had to watch the husband have sex with the other wives for several nights. When he finally had intercourse with her, the others watched.

This lack of modesty is in total contrast to the more demure China of today. A recent study found that eighty-seven percent of Chinese couples only make love with their clothes on. What could be less intimate?

What cultures thought the feet were the most sensuous female attribute?

A limited number of men entertain a fetish for feet today, but in some cultures all men adored the female foot. The most notable example were the Chinese. In this ancient culture, for a female to be sexually desirable, her feet had to be bound from a young age, rendering them tiny and essentially useless for walking. This nonsense got started during the Sung dynasty (960–976 A.D.), when a palace dancer with tiny feet wrapped in silk ribbons wowed the court. Her popularity led to the disfigurement of millions of little girls over the centuries that followed.

Before a girl turned five, all toes but her first were broken. They were then bent back under the sole of the foot and tightly bound, while the heel was brought forward. The practice is said to have been extremely painful and potentially dangerous, as gangrene was a common side effect. The ideal foot size, called the Golden Lotus, was around three inches. The feet were then considered to be so erotic that even the husband was not allowed to see his wife barefooted.

Western society may find this gross deformity hideous, but

Chinese men of the time thought a wife with small nonfunctional feet was a status symbol because it showed he was wealthy enough to have a wife who didn't do any work. The practice continued well into the twentieth century. Today in China, thirty-eight percent of women aged eighty or older have bound feet.

The Spanish men of the 1600s also had a thing about a woman's feet. Size wasn't important though, just the mere sight of a woman's shoe was enough to be scandalous. Women wore full-length body cloaks called *tapados* that covered everything but their left eye. The tapados always reached to the ground to hide the feet. Special carriages were even built with doors that concealed the feet when getting in and out.

The most common modern fetish is that of the foot. Some speculate that because a mother's feet is the first thing a crawling baby sees before being picked up and suckled, the foot becomes associated with loving and nurturing.

How was garlic used to test a woman's fertility?

The poor women of days gone by. They had everything from A to Z inserted into their vaginas, for one reason or another. Sixteenth-century maidens put cloves of garlic inside themselves to check their fertility. If after twelve hours the garlic odor was detectable on their breath, so the thinking went, they were fertile.

Why did Egyptian women urinate on wheat seeds?

Most women have one of two reactions to learning that they are pregnant: elation or horror. It has always been this way, and people have been trying to test for pregnancies since ancient times.

Pregnancy tests were given as long ago as 2,000 B.C. Egyptian doctors had a rather interesting test procedure. They told the woman to place barley and wheat seeds in a cloth and urinate on it daily. If both seeds germinated, she was pregnant. If the highly-prized wheat seed germinated first, she would be blessed with a son. If the lowly barley seed sprouted first, she would give birth to a girl, considered less desirable.

While this test was totally unreliable, it is interesting that they made the connection between pregnancy and some kind of change in the urine. Today's at-home pregnancy tests use the same approach. Unfortunately, they still can't predict the sex of the child.

How can a fish be used to test for pregnancy?

Another odd pregnancy test of more recent times was the "Bitterling test." It was a nineteenth-century Eastern European pregnancy test that involved putting a small carp-like fish in a quart of water containing two teaspoons of the woman's urine. The hormones in her urine caused the oviducts of the fish to descend if she were pregnant. (Not quite as convenient as the E.P.T.)

Can you name two reasons for placing a fish in a woman's vagina?

The things some people will do for sex! As a means of stirring their man's desires, some English wives in the Middle Ages placed a live fish in their vagina until it died. Then it was cooked and served to their indifferent husband. The horny housewife might also make a loaf of bread on which she had made an impression of her vulva before baking.

In more modern times, the men of the Ponapean culture are said to place a fish in the vulva of their mate and gently lick it out before intercourse.

What culture actually built a temple in honor of the buttocks?

It had to be the Greeks. The Greeks revered the female backside, even more so than the breasts. It was quite common for the women of ancient Greece to pad their bottoms to achieve a fuller look. Such was the Greek reverence for the buttocks, that they actually dedicated a temple to honor them, "Aphrodite

Kallipygeia," meaning "Aphrodite of the Great Ass." The temple was not built by some offbeat cult, but was actually part of the official state religion.

Was there ever a gay pope?

With all the gay priests running around these days, it should come as no surprise that there have been a number of gay popes over the years. Holy men have not always run the Catholic Church. As a matter of fact, during the Middle Ages and the Renaissance, the position of pope was often a political appointment. The office could be bought by the wealthy or controlled by a powerful Italian family and passed from generation to generation. Celibacy was not always foremost in these politicos minds. Thus we now know that several popes fathered children, were bisexual, or even gay.

Among the popes believed to be bisexual or gay were:

- John XII, who was bisexual and reigned form 705 to 708.
- Benedict IX, who was a homosexual and sat on the throne from 1032 to 1045.
- Alexander VI, a bisexual who fathered eight children and served from 1254 to 1261.
- Paul II, who sat from 1464 to 1471, was probably a transsexual and was known as "Our Lady of Pity" because of his affinity for women's clothing.
- Sixtus IV, a homosexual who followed Paul II from 1471 to 1484.
- Leo X, who was a bisexual and served from 1513 to 1521.

Priests and popes were not required to be celibate until the eleventh century. Before that, the Church had a more lenient view on sex and there were many married popes.

Was there ever a pregnant pope?

This is one of those "truth is stranger than fiction" stories, if it is to be believed. According to historical documents (Bartolomeo

Platina's *Lives of the Popes*, 1479), a woman actually became pope in 855 A.D. As the story goes, John VIII, of English stock though born in Mentz, became pope through "magical arts." A woman, she disguised herself as a man from a young age. She traveled to Greece where she studied intensely. When she later went to Rome, few could match her knowledge of the Scriptures. Her public readings and dissertations there earned her a great following, which included Pope Leo IV. Such was the respect for her at the Vatican that she was appointed pope upon Leo's death.

After she became pope, she slept with one of her male servants and became pregnant. She managed to hide her condition until the day she went into labor while walking to the Lateran Church. She died on the spot, halfway between the Colosseum and St. Clement's. She had been pope for two years, one month, and four days at her death. The Church kept things quiet, burying her with very little pomp.

Whether the story is entirely accurate or not, it does help to explain one unusual ritual that new popes were subjected to for centuries. Upon their first seating in the porphyry chair, the youngest deacon would reach his hand up through a hole in the seat and feel the Pope's testicles. Not only did this ensure his manhood, but this ritual also served the purpose of reminding the pope that he is human, not God-like, and subject to the call of nature. Hence the chair was referred to as the "Sedes Stercoraria," or "Fecal Throne."

What saint had her breasts cut off?

There is not a lot of information about this martyr. Born in Catania, Italy, Agatha (born?–died A.D. 251) was a young, pretty, rich Christian girl, who led a life devoted to God. The local magistrate, Quinctianus, was a feared persecutor of Christians. He tried to blackmail Agatha into having sex with him in exchange for not prosecuting her. When she refused, he had her sent to a brothel and beaten. When she refused to accept customers, or Quinctianus, he had her breasts cut off and left her to bleed to death. In a vision, St. Peter came to her and dressed her wounds. Agatha survived, only to be stretched on the rack and then rolled in hot coals. During her torture, an earthquake struck, scaring off her tormenters. Agatha thanked God for ending her pain, and she died.

Legend has it that carrying her death veil in a procession will keep Mt. Etna from erupting. She is now the patron saint for preventing volcanic eruption. She is also the patron saint for breast diseases, rape victims, and wet nurses. Agatha's representation is breasts on a dish and her feast day is February 5th.

When did European men openly display their genitals in public?

The open display of a man's genitals is one of the last fashion taboos in the modern world. This, however, was not the case in thirteenth-century Europe. Far from being taboo, the noblemen of the 1200s were as proud as peacocks when it came to their members. The genitals were fashionably displayed through a hole in the crotch of their tights. The short tunics of the day did not obstruct their splendor. The unfortunate nobleman who was not so well-endowed often chose to wrap his package in a *braquette*, which was a padded, flesh-colored, false penis made of leather.

The more modest men of the fourteenth, fifteenth, and sixteenth centuries preferred the codpiece, a protective penis sheath (*cod* is an Old English word meaning "scrotum"). The codpiece was originally a metal piece of crotch armor worn by knights in battle. As a fashion statement, it was worn with tight breeches, stuffed, and ornately decorated. One practical reason for the stuffing of one's tights was to prevent the penis from popping out of the fly (men wore no underwear in those days). Strategically placed cloths did the trick. The cloths also served a second purpose: Tights did not have pockets, so the codpiece was a convenient place to keep coins, keys, or what have you.

The codpiece eventually evolved to a point were it protruded straight out at lengths of up to five inches. The Church condemned them as "fashions of the Devil." The double-stitched trouser fly of today is a remnant of the codpieces of old.

Why did some people used to marry trees?

The idea that someone would marry a tree sounds crazy. Even the most ardent dendrologist (tree expert) would probably prefer a human spouse. However, such a weird ritual was practiced by the Brahman men of southern India. Their law required that among brothers, the eldest had to marry first. If the older brother remained unwed for one reason or another, the younger brothers were stuck. A little loophole in the law was for the older brother to marry a tree, in what is known as a "mock marriage."

The Punjab were another Indian culture that permitted marriage to trees. Punjabis believed that if a widower married for the third time, his new wife would have to be protected from any evil spirits that may have killed the first two. In order to trick the spirits, the widower underwent a mock marriage to a tree or sheep dressed up like a woman. It was hoped that the evil forces would kill the surrogate bride, not the human one.

What did belly dancing have to do with sex education?

Belly dancing originated in Turkey, Greece, Egypt, and Africa. It was performed as a religious dance of sex and childbirth. In Egypt, belly dancing was used as a kind of sex education lesson for young couples. Called *awalem*, this type of dance showed newlyweds how to move their bodies during lovemaking. The modern belly dance was first brought to the United States by impressario Sol Bloom at the 1893 Chicago World's Fair (Bloom also gave it the name "belly dance"). Today, belly-dance movements don't have a sexual significance. They simply are an exotic art form that teases and entertains.

Did there really used to be chastity belts?

Yes, Virginia, some women really were shackled in belts to ensure chastity in our dark past. Some claim that the chastity belt is a nineteenth-century creation, but there is evidence that they first came on the scene in fifteenth-century Italy, probably as a protection against rape. Gradually, they came to be used to ensure the fidelity of promiscuous wives.

Originally called "the Girdle of Venus" or "the Florentine Girdle," the typical chastity belt had a metal strap that fit up between the legs and locked around the hips. It had two holes with sharp outward-facing metal teeth, which permitted elimination but not penetration. Later, in the nineteenth century, chastity belts were used on members of both sexes to prevent masturbation. The male version was usually some sort of a harness that held the penis in such a way as to prevent an erection. Again, metal teeth or spikes were often involved.

The idea for such a contraption is said to have come from Homer's *Odyssey*. The story goes that Hephaistos, Aphrodite's husband, forged a girdle to curb her infidelity. Chastity belts continued to be sold in medical catalogs until the 1930s.

Today, chastity belts are for fun and eighty percent of them are worn by males. The man's partner can lock up his penis in one of these modern belts and keep the key. This transfers a lot of power to the key holder, which some people find to be a turn on.

Is castration mentioned in the Bible?

Castration was so common in ancient times that it is even mentioned in the Bible. In the Book of Samuel, King Saul, who wanted David to be killed, agreed to let him marry his daughter Michal. In 1 Samuel 18:27, Saul's officials tell David, "All the king wants from you in payment for the bride are the foreskins of one hundred dead Philistines. . . ." It was Saul's plan that David would be killed by the Philistines.

What army used to castrate their vanquished opponents?

As far back as 2,000 B.C., Middle Eastern armies castrated their defeated foes for trophies. This was not only a humiliating practice, but also one that provided numerous docile slaves. The removal of the testicles effectively reduces the production of testosterone, thus pacifying the slaves and causing them to become more feminine in appearance. In 1300 B.C., King Menephta returned to Egypt after defeating the Libyans with more than 13,000 phalli removed from his foes. A stone monument in Karnak lists the inventory of his trophies:

—Phalli of Libyan generals: 6
—Phalli cut off Libyans: 6,359
—Sirculians killed, phalli cut off: 222
—Etruscans killed, phalli cut off: 542
—Greeks killed, phalli presented to the king: 6,111

The castration of defeated foes was not only limited to the ancient world. In some Native American cultures, the squaws of the victorious tribesmen cut off the genitals of the conquered.

What culture's ladies enjoyed having sex slaves?

Castration was not just reserved for those defeated in battle. Living castrati (eunuchs) were also in great demand. The Romans enjoyed the services of *spadones*: men who had their testicles removed but retained the penis. A Roman woman's prestige was enhanced by the number of these soft, beardless sex slaves who attended to her every whim. A spado enabled the ladies to copulate all they wanted without the fear of pregnancy.

Roman men also enjoyed the company of eunuchs. Being hairless and soft, with large firm breasts, these androgynous men (called *voluptas* because of their feminine shape) were very appealing to many affluent Roman men. So popular was the practice of pedophilia with young eunuchs that emperor Domitian had to pass a law fixing a lower age limit (seven years old) for castrating or prostituting boys in 84 A.D. What a benevolent leader!

What are "eunuchs"?

The word "eunuch" comes from the Latin *eunuchus* and the Greek *eunouchos*, meaning "keeper of the bedchamber." The harem, or seraglio, was the forbidden area of a sultan's house. Here lived his many wives and concubines. Virile men could not be trusted to watch over such tempting possessions. The obvious alternative was the eunuch.

Eunuchs are totally castrated (penis and testicles) men. At the height of the Byzantine Empire, as many as a thousand eunuchs might have been in service. As well as protecting the harem, these castrated men also trained uncastrated men for positions in public service, and they chose which boys were to become the eunuchs of the future.

Most countries have done away with harems, although King Hassan of Morocco, who ruled until 1999, was rumored to have had one consisting of over 200 women. They lived a secret life of seclusion, and none were allowed to bear children. Hassan's heir, Mohammed VI, married *one* woman in 2002, and says he will be a more modern ruler, observing women's rights.

When did the Catholic Church encourage castration?

Since the early days of Christianity, the Catholic Church looked for male singers with unusually high voices. They couldn't use female sopranos because St. Paul forbade them from singing in church. This prohibition lasted until the seventeenth century. As such, any church musical piece that was scored for a very high voice would use a falsetto: a prepubescent boy or a man straining to sing high.

One day (no one knows exactly when), someone realized that boys who were castrated (had their testicles removed, not their penises) would retain their high-pitched voices into manhood. The Vatican started employing the services of castrated sopranos in 1599, after Pope Clement VIII first heard one sing. While the Church went to pains to condemn the practice of castration, they nevertheless hired castrati (as they were called) to sing in the Vatican chapel and cathedrals. In fact, the Vatican Chapel choir used them up until the twentieth century, although Pope Leo XIII forbade the hiring of new castrati in 1878.

The practice of castrating boys became totally acceptable in Italy by the eighteenth century. Castrati were highly-prized by opera companies. A successful soprano could become very rich. As a consequence, many poor Italian families with a young son possessing an exceptional soprano voice would have him castrated in hopes of his becoming a big star in adulthood. Most did not.

How was castration performed?

Pity the poor slave or sex offender who was selected for castration. First, he was held or strapped down. A piece of twine was usually tied tightly around the base of his penis and scrotum. A sharp knife or razor was used to slice off his genitals. The wound was immediately cauterized with a red-hot poker or molten tar. Ouch!

Water was withheld from the castrated man for several days, as urination would cause infection. After the wound had somewhat healed over, the new eunuch was forced to drink copious amounts of water, with the hope that when he finally did urinate, a new hole would be formed somewhere in the scar tissue. Sometimes a feather was stuck in the wound after cauterizing, to provide a hole for elimination. The process was so hideously crude and traumatic that less than twenty percent ever survived the ordeal.

Were the Victorians really as prudish as we imagine?

The very word "Victorian" has come to mean "stuffy." The world of nineteenth-century England, under the rule of Queen Victoria, really *was* as prudish as you probably imagine. Maybe more so.

The average Victorian family had six children, and eighteen percent had ten or more! There was obviously no shortage of sex going on. It was just very straight-laced. Intercourse was banned during pregnancies and menses. The women seem to have been more responsible for this than the men. While the sexually conservative wives maintained control over intercourse, the men often took their pleasures elsewhere to spare their wives from their carnal desires. Prostitution boomed. During this era, there was reportedly one female prostitute for every twelve sexually active males in London.

The women were also very modest with their doctors. A woman needed a chaperone to see a physician, and gynecological exams only took place under extreme conditions. A woman would show her doctor on a doll where her pains were. In the extreme case where an actual physical examination was required, it was often conducted under a sheet in a darkened room.

What is infibulation?

So concerned were Victorian-era parents in Europe about their children masturbating or having wet dreams that they would "infibulate" them. Infibulation involved pulling the foreskin up over the penis head and either sewing it together or inserting little locking rings through the skin to hold it in place.

The Russian army used to infibulate its soldiers by sticking a wire through the foreskin and soldering a seal onto the ends to prevent tampering. Ancient Greek athletes believed that ejaculating sapped them of strength so they pulled their foreskin up over the glans and tied it off, preventing any kind of erection.

What well-respected sex researcher was quite the pervert?

Pervert is a relative term, but most of you will find Alfred Kinsey's private life to be somewhat abnormal. Not only was he a bisexual who encouraged friends to have sex with his wife, but he also enjoyed sticking things like toothbrushes into his penis, and he actually circumcised himself in the bathtub. Not really the habits one would attribute to a well-respected scientific researcher, even if his specialty was sex.

How did Alfred Kinsey get so into sex?

Kinsey suffered many childhood illnesses that left him with a curved spine and a weak heart. To compensate for his ill health, he joined the Boy Scouts and became one of America's first Eagle

Scouts. He loved the outdoors and biology. His domineering, evangelical Methodist father, however, wanted him to study engineering instead of biology. After two years of technical school, he spurned his father and left to study biology at Bowdoin College. He got a Ph.D. from Harvard University in 1919, and landed an assistant professorship at the University of Indiana, where he became a world expert on gall wasps. How exciting.

In 1937, he participated in a sex education course for married and engaged seniors at the university. It was then that Kinsey realized his true calling. He saw that there was a dearth of any scientific data in the area of human sexuality, and thus began his quest. He ended his lectures by asking the students to give him their sex histories. From then on, Kinsey was off and running. Soon, he was gathering data from other students, faculty, and anyone else who would talk to him. In 1941 he received a grant from the Rockefeller Foundation to continue his groundbreaking sexual survey.

As his study grew, so did funding and staffing. He opened the Institute for Sex Research (later renamed the Kinsey Institute) on the Indiana campus as a nonprofit organization in 1947. Most of his team were kindred spirits, and they often had sexual relationships amongst themselves. (All in the name of science, of course.)

In 1948, Kinsey took the world by surprise with the publication of his book *Sexual Behavior in the Human Male*. The work created immediate controversy with its findings on white American male sexuality. The uproar over the book guaranteed it would become a best seller; it sold 250,000 copies in a dozen different languages. Kinsey followed up this success with *Sexual Behavior in the Human Female* in 1953, which also sold about 250,000 copies. These two books dispelled many sexual myths and made it okay to talk about sex. The findings covered such taboo topics as homosexuality, bisexuality, extramarital sex, oral sex, masturbation, and prostitution.

Kinsey's findings shocked most Americans at the time. He revealed the following:

- Women enjoy sex as much as men do.
- One-half of women engage in pre-marital intercourse.
- One-quarter of women have had extramarital sex.
- One-third of men and thirteen percent of women have had homosexual sex at least once by age forty-five.
- Ten percent of American males have been homosexuals at some time, and four percent are exclusively homosexual.
- Sixty-nine percent of men have been to a prostitute.
- Ninety percent of males and sixty-two percent of females masturbate.

While Kinsey's sample methods and findings on the sexual practices of middle-class white America are somewhat suspect today, he did break the ice for other researchers and help to set the Sexual Revolution in motion.

How did Masters and Johnson get together?

William Howell Masters was born in Cleveland, Ohio, in 1915. His eventual wife and research partner, Virginia Eshelman Johnson, was born in 1925 in Springfield, Montana. A gynecologist, Masters was interested in the nature of sexuality and wanted to conduct research in this area. The way had already been paved for him by the work of Alfred Kinsey (see above).

In 1957, he hired Johnson, a psychologist, as a research assistant. They developed polygraph-like instruments that could measure and record human sexual response. Using these kinds of instruments, they observed 700 men and women having intercourse or masturbating in their laboratory.

These studies led to the publication of their book *Human Sexual Response* in 1966. The book identified and described the four sexual phases in the sexual cycle: excitement, plateau, orgasm, and resolution. America had recently come out of the sexual dark ages and the book became a best-seller. Masters and Johnson became overnight celebrities. All this watching of other people have sex together must have also stimulated the two researchers; Masters dumped his first wife and married Johnson. In 1970 they published the results of their subsequent research in *Human Sexual Inadequacy*. This book explored premature ejaculation, impotence, frigidity, and other sexual problems. The groundwork they laid in these two books formed the basis of the new field of sex therapy.

Masters and Johnson continued their research through the 1970s and 1980s. Their 1979 book *Homosexuality in Perspective* dispelled the misconception that homosexuality is some form of mental illness. Their final work, *Heterosexual Behavior in the Age of AIDS* was published in 1988. Their marriage fell apart a few years later and they divorced in 1993.

Their legacy lives on, however. In 1970, they established a Masters and Johnson clinic in St. Louis. The clinic has trained many students who went on to practice sex therapy around the country and the clinic still treats people with sexual dysfunctions today.

CHAPTER ELEVEN

Around the World in Bed

Where in the world do women have the biggest buttocks?

You ladies may be relieved to know that it is not the United States. That distinction belongs to the Hottentot people of Africa. They have a condition known as "steatopygia," where the buttocks produce copious amounts of excessive fat. It is not uncommon for members of this tribe to have buttocks with each half spanning two or three feet. The condition is also known as "Hottentot bustle." Another condition these women have is known as "Hottentot apron," which is an elongated labia minora.

Where do men prefer their ladies to have a moustache?

There's a strange village in Romania where mustaches are very popular—on the women! The gals of Baleni-Sirbi in Dimbovita County, Romania believe that mustaches are a sign of fidelity and fertility. The *Libertatea* newspaper reports that mustachioed women are the most sought after as prospective brides. The women say their facial hair signifies that they come from a special place. The men are quoted as saying, "It's a sign of fertility. Girls with a moustache are the most dutiful and always get married first."

What men always have an erection?

In our society, this would be a somewhat embarrassing predicament, but a full-time semierect penis is the status quo for the bushmen of the Kalahari. Their members are always slightly extended and firm. This is because their inner-penis cylinder is rich in super-dense, spongy erectile tissue. When they reach full erection, their penises don't get much bigger or harder.

Where in the world do men tie weights on the ends of their penises?

To the Karamojong tribe of northerneastern Uganda, a long penis is a thing of beauty. They are so determined to have as long a penis as possible that they start to tie weights on the ends of boys' penises at puberty. The amount of weight is gradually increased. A teenager may eventually end up with a twenty-pound stone disc swinging from the end of his member! Through this primitive but effective technique, their penises can be stretched to the phenomenal length of 18 inches. Sounds great, but the longer the penis gets, the thinner it gets. They end up with long, thin units that can get in the way of doing simple things, like sitting down. Thus, the men are known to tie their unwieldy penises into knots or double knots! (The young women of the Baganda culture use a similar technique to create dangling breasts.)

Where do women lengthen their labia to entice men?

For every type of body mutilation, there seems to be somewhere in the world where it will turn someone on. Such is the case with labia lengthening. The women of two different African tribes—the Benin of western Africa and the Venda of southern Africa—have the custom of stretching out their labia to great lengths. This is accomplished by constantly tugging on them or having friends tug on them. In time, they can hang down to a length of seven inches. But what does a girl do with such long dangling lips while doing the daily chores? They simply fold them up into the vagina to get them out of the way. Most convenient.

The Ponapeans of the Eastern Caroline Islands also like enlarged labia and clitori; however, they have a more painful method of achieving them. They apply stinging ants to their genitals. The things a girl must do to look attractive!

Does everybody kiss?

Kissing, in our society, is almost a prerequisite to making love. How many of us just hop in the sack and have intercourse with no preliminary kissing? It just doesn't seem natural. One reason we like to kiss is because the lips and tongue are two of the most sensitive parts of the body, packed with nerve endings. (The lips, tongue, and genitals all have unique skin receptors, called Krause's corpuscle, that are sensitive to pressure). In fact, there are women who can achieve an orgasm from kissing alone. As you might suspect, kissing is quite common in most other parts of the world. Ninety percent of the world's peoples kiss. The Somali are an exception. Kissing was not part of their culture before Western contact. Other peoples, like the Thonga of South Africa, are actually repulsed by it. All cultures, however, make some sort of facial contact before sex—rubbing noses, blowing, patting, licking, etc. The Eskimos are known for their nose-rubbing. In actuality, they press their nose and mouth against one another's cheeks and inhale. The word for "kissing" and "smelling" are the same in some Eskimo languages. Even some of our primate cousins, such as the chimpanzees and bonobos, kiss.

One interesting footnote: England's King Henry VI outlawed kissing in 1439 because he wanted to stop the spread of disease.

Where did they sell used panties out of vending machines?

Apparently, we Americans don't have a monopoly on weird fetishes or crazy ways to make a buck. In 1993, one inventive Japanese businessman, came up with a way to further exploit the Japanese fetish for used panties. In order to meet demand for the soiled panties of young girls, this guy began selling them on suburban streets in vending machines. There was so much bad press around the world about this that the government dug up an obscure law to shut him down.

There was even a used-undie shop called Final Fantasia, where Japanese men could go and watch a schoolgirl remove her bra and panties before he bought them. The girls stood in groups behind a one-way mirror and posed for customers. They wore price tags on their bras and panties. When selected, the customer could watch the girl go into a separate room and remove her undies, to confirm that he was getting what he was paying for. The garments were placed into a basket and passed through a hole to the buyer. Soiled underwear, feces, and urine were also for sale. It is believed that at least 1,800 girls aged 15 and older worked at the establishment.

Why did the French invent the bidet?

The bidet originated in France sometime around 1710, at a time when full-body bathing was done just once a week. It was invented to cleanse the privates in between regularly scheduled baths. In 1750, the bidet à seringue appeared. It had an upward spray that was controlled by a hand-operated pump. With it came a new use for the bidet.

Along with its use for personal hygiene, the bidet now was also used in birth control. French women often used a sponge to prevent pregnancies. Soaked in an astringent and tied to a string, the sponge was inserted into the vagina and pulled out after intercourse. A thorough bidet douching followed. It is also rumored that French men would be more inclined to perform cunnilingus on a freshly washed female.

The bidet never caught on in the United States. Americans tend to bathe daily, and feel no need to wash the nether regions between showers.

Where are young boys required to engage in ritual sodomy?

The Sambia of New Guinea believe that a boy must receive the semen of an older male to develop into a man. Boys aged seven to ten are taken to a "men's house" in the village, where they will live for the next ten years. Here they are made to perform oral sex on the older, teenage boys, several times a week, until they reach puberty. When the young boys develop adult genitals, they stop fellating older boys. It's then their turn to be the receivers of oral sex from the new crop of prepubescent boys. Older boys never perform oral sex. It is their job to give their semen to the youngsters, who must swallow it. The Sambia believe young boys need to receive adult warrior semen to become strong.

Another rather odd New Guinean culture is the Keraki. Older men, as a puberty ritual, sodomize young boys for a period of one year. After this one-year period, the boys will begin having anal sex with newly initiated boys to make them strong with adult semen. Using this same kind of logic, the Keraki believe that men can become pregnant unless they eat lime after anal sex. It must work. To date no Keraki men have ever been found to be pregnant!

What people bite off each other's eyebrows and eyelashes?

Talk about rough sex! The Trobriand Islanders of the South Pacific bite off their partner's eyebrows and eyelashes during sex. Not only this; they also scratch and bite other body parts and pull one another's hair, often leaving permanent scars, which they proudly display as badges of honor.

Conversely, the men of the island of Tikopia, near the Solomons, are forbidden to touch any genitals, including their own. It is the women who must guide the penis into the vagina for intercourse.

What people eat insects before sex?

Many of us enjoy food as a prelude to sex, maybe a romantic candlelit dinner or breakfast in bed. Sex for the Siriono tribe of eastern Bolivia involves consuming a snack that we might find disgusting. The sexual partners carefully groom each other to remove ticks and lice, which they eat before engaging in intercourse. This odd type of foreplay excludes any kissing or caressing before coitus. They are also one of the cultures that like fat women, especially a fat vulva. The men get so estatic about fat female genitals that they actually write songs about them. Another odd fact about the Siriono sex life is their practice of allowing sexual relations between one's spouse and one's siblings.

Where do men greet one another by shaking penises?

We in the modern Western world practice the custom of shaking hands upon meeting each other. The shaking of open hands traditionally symbolizes friendship by showing one another that no weapons are being concealed by either party and displaying a form of intimate body contact. Other cultures have different ways of conveying the same message upon meeting. The Japanese, for instance, keep their hands at their sides and lower their heads out of respect for the other. The Walibri tribe of central Australia are somewhat more friendly and intimate in their greetings than we are. When the Walibri men of different tribes meet for ceremonial functions, they shake each other's penises instead of hands. Now that's really exchanging pleasantries!

What is an "ampalling?"

Unless you live in the Philippines or Borneo, you probably won't know this one. The men in parts of these countries make a small cut in the skin of their penis, which they keep open during healing by inserting an oiled dove feather. The purpose of this hole is not one of decoration, but one of pleasure: female pleasure, that is.

Before intercourse, the men can insert an "ampalling," a two-inch rod made of gold or ivory. The top of the rod has a small knob that is left exposed during intercourse. It is said to greatly stimulate the female partner.

Other sex aids enjoyed by Southeast Asians are gold or silver nuggets inserted just below the skin of the penis. They are called "tickling stones." Some of the men of Burma prefer inserting little metal bells, referred to as "Burmese bells." Such men can sometimes be identified by the faint tinkling sound they make when they walk around.

Why do some men willingly cut off their testicles?

Some African tribes believe that by cutting off one testicle and burning it in offering to their gods, his fertility will be increased. The Hottentots of southern Africa believe that having twins is an evil omen, so they cut off one of a man's testicles before he is to conceive. (Good plan.) Apparently they believe that two testicles might produce two children. The Ponapeans require a boy to have a testicle removed as a rite of puberty.

What is a "love apple?"

During Shakespearean times, young maidens would place a peeled apple under their arms until it acquired their own unique individual aroma. They would then present it to the "apple" of their eye to be consumed.

Similar customs are still practiced today. In the Balkans and Greece, men place handkerchiefs in their armpits at dances and offer them to prospective partners. Engaged couples in parts of the Phillipines carry about articles of their future partners' soiled underwear to sniff and caress during times apart.

Some Caribbean peoples concoct a love potion made from ground meat cooked in their own sweat, which they serve to the object of their desire. If that isn't unappealing enough for you, the Siwi men of North Africa secretly put some of their semen into a woman's food to cast their spell over her. Yummy!

CHAPTER TWELVE

You Can't Do That!

Why couldn't nuns eat beans?

No, it's not because of that! The real reason is even sillier. In the fourth century A.D., Saint Jerome, who believed that foods shaped like genitals were aphrodisiacs, forbade nuns from eating beans. Supposedly, he thought their shape somewhat resembled testicles, and that they exuded a liquid that made people horny. It sounds as if St. Jerome was the one with the dirty mind!

Why aren't ministers celibate?

Any happily married minister can thank Martin Luther for his or her marital bliss. Luther, as you may know, was an Augustinian monk in the sixteenth century. He became fed up with many aspects of the Catholic Church, including the failure of priests and popes to keep their vow of celibacy.

The Catholic Church didn't always require its clergy to take a vow of celibacy. In the fourth century, St. Augustine wrote that marriage was okay if the man felt he had to have sex, but celibacy was more holy. Later, the Church adopted the celibacy requirement, but then as now, many priests and even popes didn't respect their vows. Martin Luther started the Protestant reformation in 1517 and disavowed the mandate that the clergy were to remain celibate. Luther saw marriage as divinely ordained and as a gift from God. As such, he married a nun and fathered seven children.

One effect of his great reverence for marriage was an intolerance for prostitution. The Catholic Church didn't come down hard on prostitution because they regarded it as a necessary evil. Martin Luther, however, viewed it simply as a threat to marriage. Thus, Protestant countries tended to be more hostile to the working girl.

Who defined sodomy?

The word "sodomy" is taken from the homosexual proclivities of the men of Sodom, mentioned in the Bible at Genesis 19:1-11. The first person to define the word "sodomy" was St. Peter Damien, in the eleventh century. He considered masturbation, anal sex, and bestiality to be sins, and felt a bureaucracy was needed to enforce laws against such behavior. His *Book of Gomorroh* is considered one of the most powerful denouncements of same-sex behavior written in the Middle Ages.

Damien brought accusations against priests for having same-sex relations with their spiritual advisers. Many of these priests avoided penalties by confessing to other gay priests who saw nothing wrong with their activities. When Damien asked Pope Leo IX to remove the offending clerics, the pope ruled that priests who had not participated in "long-standing practice or with many men" should remain in the priesthood. Those who were extremely sinful would be lowered in rank.

The definition of sodomy was later expanded by Thomas Aquinas in the thirteenth century to include lesbianism, any non-vaginal sex, and even marital sex with the woman on top.

Why did men in Europe used to have their penises nailed to a stake?

If you think society is rough on homosexuals today, just be glad you didn't live in sixteenth-century Europe. The punishment for being caught in a homosexual act was to be nailed to a stake by your penis in the town square for twenty-four hours, and then taken out and burned alive. Acts of sodomy were still capital crimes in England until 1861, when the punishment was changed to life in prison. The Puritan settlers in Connecticut also imposed capital punishment for homosexuality, as well as for adultery and bestiality.

By the late eighteenth century, more forward-thinking people, like Thomas Jefferson, suggested merely castrating homosexuals. By the early nineteenth century, a jail sentence of a few years was common in England, but not before putting the accused on public display in the pillory, where all kinds of foul objects were hurled their way. By the time of the most famous sodomy trial of the late nineteenth century, Oscar Wilde's, the punishment was just two years of hard labor.

Eight countries still have the death penalty for homosexuality—Afghanistan, Iran, Mauritania, Pakistan, Saudi Arabia, Sudan, United Arab Emirates, and Yemen.

Big changes recently occurred that will make life much easier for homosexuals or anyone else who enjoys sodomy in America. On June 26, 2003, the United States Supreme Court, in a 6–3 decision, reversed a seventeen-year-old ruling that allowed states to punish people who engaged in sodomy. The Court found that laws that make same-sex intercourse a crime violate the due-process clause of the Fourteenth Amendment. This ruling gives every American a right to sexual privacy for the first time.

Up until 1960, every state had some kind of antisodomy law. At the time of the ruling, nine states—Alabama, Florida, Idaho, Louisiana, Mississippi, North Carolina, South Carolina, Utah, and Virginia—had laws banning consensual sodomy for everyone, while Texas, Kansas, Oklahoma, and Missouri had laws criminalizing oral or anal sex between same-sex couples only.

What were some of the bizarre forms of punishment for adultery?

Most major cultures throughout history have frowned upon adultery. Generally, it was the woman who suffered the most severe consequences. Death sentences were, and still are, carried out in some countries. Short of death, there were many weird and wild punishments meted out.

A European woman could have her ears and nose cut off to mark her transgression. The Zulu had a custom of shoving a cactus up the vagina of an adulteress. The Vietnamese punished an adulteress by having an elephant trample her to death. Stoning to death is practiced to this day in Nigeria and Saudi Arabia, and adultery is still a capital offense for women in Iran, Pakistan, and Yemen.

One of the weirder punishments for an adulterer was the ancient Roman punishment of sticking a spiny-headed fish up his anus. Another ancient punishment seems almost humorous: The Greeks would pluck the pubic hair from an adulterer and stick a large radish into his anus!

What country routinely performed virginity tests on high school girls until 2002?

The Islamic nation of Turkey just ceased a practice that we in the West would find intolerable. High school girls who were suspected of premarital sex were forced to submit to a gynecological examination to determine if their virginity was still intact. Many girls found the idea so abhorrent that they would attempt suicide with rat poison rather than undergoing the ordeal. Female applicants for certain jobs and university students were forced to suffer the same kind of humiliation. More progressive thinkers finally won sway in February 2002, and the practice was finally officially banned. However, it remains to be seen if the new laws are enforced.

Is it illegal to photograph up a woman's skirt without asking?

This one's a no-brainer, right? Wrong. The Washington State Supreme Court ruled on September 19, 2002 that it is not a crime to take pictures up women's skirts in public places! The high court ruled on two cases of men who were arrested in 1999 and 2000. In the 1999 case, Sean Glas, 28, was caught by an employee of the Valley Mall's Sears store in Union Gap, Washington, after she noticed, out of the corner of her eye, a flash around her backside and saw Glas crouched down low with a camera, shooting up her skirt. Glas told police that while what he did was immoral, he didn't believe it to be illegal. Apparently he was right. His intent was to sell the pictures to an Internet site that specializes in such voyeurism.

Justice Bobbe Bridge, one of four women on the state supreme court, wrote in the unanimous opinion, "Although [their] actions are reprehensible, we agree that the voyeurism statute, as written, does not prohibit up-skirt photography in a public place." The prosecution and defense attorneys both agreed that this ruling will almost certainly lead the legislature to change the law. So mind your skirts in Washington for now, ladies.

As this book is going to press, laws are being introduced to make this practice illegal.

In what country are women forbidden from entering a church while menstruating?

Throughout history and right up until the present day, many societies have considered a menstruating woman as unclean and taboo. Many tribal cultures still think a woman is possessed by evil spirits during her period and that she should keep away from others. Sex with a menstruating woman was thought to result in deformed babies, diseases in the man's sex organs, or loss of virility. Happily, this taboo has been removed in most of the modern world, but not all.

For example, in the predominately Hindu country of Bali, women are not to enter a temple if menstruating. In India, Brahman women are to keep separate for four days and not be touched. If anyone comes in contact with them, they must bathe at once. The disdain of a woman's period is also still found in some Christian countries, like Greece, where not only are menstruating women barred from church, but they are also prohibited from receiving communion, baking bread, or making wine.

In parts of Greece, a woman is also considered unclean for forty days after she has given birth. During this time period she is to stay confined and is not allowed to enter a church. The roots of such foolishness can be traced back to the Old Testament.

In case you thought there wasn't a museum for everything somewhere in this world, the Museum of Menstruation opened in Hyattsville, Maryland in 1994.

How old do you have to be to get married?

During the Victorian era, the legal age of consent was only ten years old in as many as twenty-five states. In Delaware, it was just seven! This seems out of step with the otherwise repressive attitudes toward sex that dominated the era. It wasn't until 1886, after a public outcry, that all but five states raised the age of legal consent to thirteen or fourteen. As late as 1930, twelve states allowed boys as young as fourteen and girls as young as twelve to marry, with parental consent.

Today, all states require couples to be at least eighteen or older to get married without parental consent. Many states waive the age requirement if the girl is pregnant or already has a child, but the couple may still need court approval.

Men in certain cultures prefer a bride fairly close to their own age. Others, however, like their wives to be much younger. Americans, Western Europeans, and Australian men look to marry a girl who is less than two years younger than they are. In Iran, Columbia, Nigeria, and Zambia, men want women at least four years younger.

Who is the world's greatest bigamist?

Some men really know how to sweep women off their feet. One amazing example of this talent is Giovanni Vigliotto from Siracusa, Sicily. Mr. Vigliotto has the dubious distinction of fraudulently marrying some one hundred and four women over a span of forty-one years, from 1949 to 1981. His victims were spread out across twenty-seven states and fourteen different countries. Incredibly, this consummate Don Juan actually managed to wed four different women on a cruise ship in 1968. The party ended for

Vigliotta on March 28, 1983, when a Phoenix, Arizona, court sentenced him to twenty-eight years in prison for fraud and six years for bigamy.

Men aren't the only ones out there committing bigamy. There is the case of Theresa Vaughn. At the tender age of twenty-four, she admitted to an English court that she had wed sixty-one different men in England, Germany, and South Africa in a five-year period.

Who was convicted of committing the most rapes on record?

Haj Muhammad Mustapha Tabet of Morocco was found guilty of raping 518 women over the course of seven years. The fifty-four-year-old police chief even videotaped the assaults. Eleven of his police colleagues were charged with obstruction of justice and destroying evidence. He was convicted on March 15, 1993 and executed by firing squad five months later.

Why did East German rapists used to grow breasts?

Before the fall of the Berlin Wall, convicted rapists in East Germany were in for a weird and wild detention. To curb their libido, many had a slow but steady flow of estrogen released into their bodies via subdermal implants. These hormonally altered men began to grow large fleshy breasts with female-like nipples and areolae. Some even were capable of lactation. Their hips and buttocks also became more curvaceous. As a result, these onetime rapists become so feminine that other male inmates started raping them. Talk about poetic justice!

In earlier times, the common punishment for rape was much harsher: castration. The Romans would crush the testicles of a first-time offender and castrate after a second offense. The Greeks would literally *pull* the testicles off of a rapist. In France, this form of punishment was used up until the time of Napoleon.

There is one health benefit to being castrated. Removal of the testicles in your twenties or thirties can extend your lifespan. Studies of the above-mentioned inmates found that, on average, a castrated prisoner outlived his intact fellow convicts by a good thirteen years. Apparently testosterone is not all that great for a man as he gets older. While being castrated offers an impressive health benefit, it is not a trade-off many men would be willing to make. Not voluntarily, anyway.

Where can you buy rape insurance?

It's nothing to boast about, but South Africa holds that dubious distinction. Officially, the police report about 64,000 sexual assaults a year. That is an incidence rate of 116 for every 100,000. While this may sound high, some officials believe the actual numbers to be several times higher—particularly devestating, in an area of the world with one of the highest levels of HIV infection. The situation is so bad that one can actually purchase rape insurance. The policies cover HIV testing and treatment, as well as counseling and help in pressing criminal charges against the assailant.

What are some obscure sex laws still on the books?

Those crazy Victorians thought that epilepsy was the result of a state of continuous sexual arousal, and that seizures were some form of sexual release. Their cure was simple: Castrate the male epileptics. This was considered such good advice that in New Jersey and Wisconsin the practice was legal into the twentieth century. What other bizarre sex laws are still on the books?

- In Florida, it is illegal to have sex with a porcupine (they need a law for this?!)
- In Fairbanks, Alaska, it is illegal for moose to copulate on the sidewalk.
- In Alexandria, Minnesota, it is illegal to have sex with your wife if your breath smells of garlic, onions, or sardines. (So much for the pizza with everything.)
- In Willowdale, Oregon, you can't talk dirty in your wife's ear.
- In Nevada, it is illegal to cheat on your spouse without using a condom.

- In Harrisburg, Pennsylvania, it is illegal to have sex with a truck driver in a toll booth (even if the trucker is out of change).
- In San Francisco (of all places), oral sex is illegal.
- In Washington, D.C., only the missionary position is legal (however, giving it to the rest of the country up the wazoo seems to be okay).

What crazy foreign sex laws have existed?

- The Germanic Teutons of A.D. 100 punished prostitutes by suffocating them in excrement.
- In Lebanon, it is illegal to have sex with a male goat, but it's okay to do it with a female goat.
- Many Middle Eastern Islamic countries forbid eating a lamb with which you have had sex.
- During the Middle Ages, bestiality wasn't viewed as favorably; offenders were burned alive, along with the animal.
- Victorian women could be jailed for not having sex with their husbands. (Maybe this one's not so crazy.)

CHAPTER THIRTEEN

Sexcetera

How much sex is going on out there?

The World Health Organization, which is charged with monitoring global reproduction, estimates that each day some 100 million people engage in acts of sexual intercourse, resulting in about 910,000 conceptions and 350,000 cases of sexually transmitted disease. Many of these conceptions are unwanted. There are around 150,000 abortions performed daily, one-third of them under adverse conditions, resulting in about 500 deaths.

How long do orgasms take?

If you are reading this book, odds are you've had an orgasm. (Otherwise, please close the book and give it back to Mommy or Daddy.) But did you ever time one as it happened? As you can probably guess by now, there are researchers who are actually paid to sit around and watch couples copulate with wires and probes attached to them. Masters and Johnson come immediately to mind. They found that the average male orgasm lasts around six to ten seconds, and the average female orgasm lasts about eight to ten seconds, with contractions occurring about every 0.8 seconds.

There are exceptions, of course. Some men can have a twenty-second orgasm, and some lucky women can go thirty seconds. There have been reports of extremely rare cases of women having orgasms lasting thirty minutes!

How many orgasms can people have in a row?
Alfred Kinsey was another bedroom busybody. He reported that some men are capable of six to eight orgasms in one session, while some women can have virtually continuous orgasms. The record for orgasms achieved in an hour goes to a woman who had one hundred thirty-four, and a man who managed sixteen! This is according to the good folks at the Center for Marital and Sexual Studies in Long Beach, California.

What is "sex flush"?
When making love, many younger people get a pink rash on the front of their body. This phenomenon occurs in seventy-five percent of women and fifty percent of men. Women get this flush on their breasts, abdomen, and upper chest, while the men get it from the face down to the stomach and buttocks. The rash is caused by increased blood flow to certain areas of the body when sexually aroused, and it is more noticeable on fair-skinned individuals. Once climax is reached, the rash disappears within about five minutes.

Does sex give you the sniffles?
You may be an acrobatic lover or a passive one, but odds are you breathe heavily through your mouth during orgasm. Whether your performance is strenuous or not, sexual arousal causes the blood vessels in your genitals, as well as in your nose, to expand. This does wonders for your penis, but reduces air flow through the nasal passages. To compensate for the restricted nasal airflow, you breathe heavily through your mouth as orgasm approaches.
Some people also get the sniffles, known as "honeymoon rhinitis," during sex. Don't worry; you're not allergic to sex. This phenomenon is caused by the added stimulation of the mucous membranes. After an orgasm, the blood is pumped away from the nose, returning things to normal.

Does sex give you a headache?

Women are more likely to use a headache as an excuse to avoid sex, but men are more likely to get a headache from having sex. A German study recently found that men are three times more likely to get a headache from having an orgasm than women. The headaches strike at the point of orgasm and can be quite severe. The condition, known as "orgasmic cephalgia," affects at least one in a hundred people during their lifetime, but some suffer on a regular basis. The headaches are believed to be brought on by the sudden increase in blood flow and dilation of the blood vessels during sex. Those afflicted are typically between the ages of twenty and twenty-five. Sexual headaches usually appear in the span of a few weeks and cease occurring spontaneously. Sufferers find that they can lessen the pain by gradually increasing their sexual excitement.

Now there's a new excuse for avoiding sex: "Not tonight dear, I'm *going* to have a headache!"

Can sex cause a heart attack?

Scientists report that vigorous sex sessions are no more likely to cause a heart attack than climbing a flight of stairs. Cardiologists now claim the risks of a heart attack during sex have been overstated in past studies. Many men at risk of a heart attack reduce sexual activity or give it up altogether. Less than one percent of all heart attacks are caused by having sex. Even for people with heart disease, the odds of having an attack during or immediately after sex is just 1 in 50,000. Apparently, if you can make it upstairs to the bedroom, you are probably okay to give it a try.

In fact, according to a study published in the *British Medical Journal*, having one hundred orgasms a year can reduce a man's chances of suffering a fatal coronary by thirty-six percent.

What is "sleep sex"?

It's kind of like sleep walking, except that you perform sex acts on yourself or your partner while sound asleep. The condition was reported by Stanford University researchers in the journal

Psychosomatic Medicine. It can range in severity from simply moaning to aggressive, and sometimes violent, sexual advances on your partner. In one case, a patient tried to strangle his wife. Another patient broke two fingers while trying to escape from restraints he had tied on himself to prevent this behavior.

The researchers believe sleep sex is caused by a sleeping disorder combined with emotional problems. Instead of passing through the five normal phases of sleep, each of which have classic brainwave patterns, patients affected by sleep sex have abnormal patterns in one of their phases. While many sleepwalkers and sleeptalkers show similar unusual brainwave patterns, it is believed the associated emotional problems cause sleep sex. Many of the patients studied had a history of sleepwalking. The condition can be cured with sleep-disorder treatment drugs similar to Valium and by using breathing disorder treatments.

What is "witches' milk"?

Some baby boys are born with swollen breasts that may exude a sweet, whitish fluid known as "witches' milk." Midwives in the days of yore used to collect this stuff for its supposed magical properties. It was said to cure infertility, as well as a host of other sexual problems.

The reason for this male production of milk is that newborns are still under the hormonal influence of their mothers for several days. These maternal hormones in the baby boy's blood can cause the glands in his breasts to lactate for up to a week.

How many of us answer the phone during sex?

It happens to all of us—you're right in the middle of making passionate love and the phone rings. A great deal about your personal priorities can be revealed by this situation. Do you carry on with the intimate business at hand, which means so much to your partner, or does curiosity get the better of you?

Each of us has our own opinion on the matter, but apparently most of us would rather be on the phone than on our partner.

According to a survey mentioned in *Playboy* magazine, sixty-five percent of women and sixty percent of men answer the phone during sex. Of those who answer the phone, twenty percent of the women and twelve percent of the men continue to have sex while talking. How many muffle the sounds of their lovemaking is unknown.

What famous children's author was also a pedophile?

What children's tale is more beautiful and magical than *Alice's Adventures in Wonderland*? Lewis Carroll, author of the timeless children's classic, was quite fond of prepubescent girls. Perhaps Carroll was a little too fond of young girls. He reportedly spent inordinate amounts of time alone with them and often photographed them in the nude.

The love of an adolescent girl by an adult is termed nymphophilia. While we may find it immoral today, up until the 1800s, the age of consent for common-law marriages was between ten and thirteen years of age in the United States.

Is it dangerous to brush your teeth before oral sex?

Many of us feel obliged to brush our teeth prior to sex. However, if you don't know your partner all that well, it may not be a good idea. *Sexuality Today* warns against brushing and flossing before oral sex, as these practices can cause tiny cuts or tears on the gums. If your partner is carrying a sexually transmitted disease, you can become infected through the gums.

This is probably good advice for those of you who indulge in one-night stands, but if you are married, or have a longtime partner, you would be better off brushing or gargling, if you really want to get any.

Does saliva kill HIV?

HIV is much less likely to be transmitted when infected semen enters the mouth than the vagina. Both are very similar physiologically. However, only the mouth contains saliva.

One unique thing about saliva is that it is the only fluid the body produces that is salt-free. The white blood cells that HIV infects contain salt. When these cells are placed in salt-free saliva, they burst, killing the HIV inside. So, while not impossible, it is much harder to get HIV from oral sex.

This does NOT mean unprotected oral sex is completely safe. It is NOT!

Is "deep-throating" dangerous?

The farther down you take a man's penis in your mouth during oral sex, the greater the pleasure he will feel, but it also results in a greater risk of HIV infection. There are cells, known as CD4+ Langerhans, that are found in the mucous membranes of the body. These cells are considered "target" or "doorway" cells for HIV. The virus seeks out CD4+ Langerhans cells as easy ways to gain entry to, and infect the body. More of these HIV-susceptible cells are found at the surface of the tissues that line the throat than on the tissues that line the mouth.

What cities have the most single people?

Looking for a mate? You may want to take note of which American cities have the most eligible partners. Certain cities have more than their fair share of single people, while others have slim pickings. The capital of the singles scene is the nation's capital—Washington, D.C.—where two out of three people are single. Other cities have the following ratios: Detroit—one in three, Los Angeles—one in four, Philadelphia—one in four, Chicago—one in five, Houston—one in six, and New York—one in seven.

Why aren't there more topless beaches in the United States?

Simply put, we don't want them. Well, the women don't want them anyway. Unlike some of our European cousins (particularly the French), who think topless beaches are perfectly natural, we Americans are not as comfortable with our bodies.

When asked, only eighteen percent of American women say they favor topless beaches. A mere six percent say they would actually go topless if allowed. Predictably, fifty percent of men favor the idea.

What city had a street called Hairy Cunt Lane?

Many centuries ago, some European streets with brothels were called by very descriptive names, which left nothing to the imagination as to what kind of business was transacted there. In fourteenth-century London, there were streets named Gropecunt Lane, Whore's Nest, and Slut's Hole. Not to be outdone, fifteenth-century Paris had such avenues as Whore's Hole Lane and Hairy Cunt Lane.

If you don't wear a seat belt, will your kids be more promiscuous?

Researchers at Southwest Texas University and the City College of New York have found a strong link between parents who engage in risky activities and teenage sex. The study included information on the sexual behavior of 19,000 adolescents between the ages of twelve and eighteen, and the smoking, drinking, and seat-belt wearing habits of one of their parents.

The researchers found that teens were more likely to have sex before age sixteen if their parents smoked or drank heavily. (Seventy percent of the women surveyed who smoke had more than four lovers a year, while sixty percent of nonsmokers had none.) They also found that boys whose parents don't wear seat belts were more likely to have sex before leaving school. Oddly, girls' sexual behavior was not affected by parental seat-belt wearing habits. So, Mom and Dad, there's one more good reason to buckle up, and to quit smoking, too.

What popular doll was modeled after a German hooker?

That's right, Barbie. The Barbie doll was designed to look just like a German sex doll, who in turn was modeled after a German newspaper's sex cartoon character. The cartoon character, named

Lilli, had a strip in the German tabloid *Bild Zeitung* in 1952. A doll version of Lilli was produced for sale to adult men in the mid-1950s.

California entrepreneur Ruth Handler, cofounder of Mattel, had been toying with the idea of introducing a more adult doll for young girls to play with, in place of the ubiquitous baby dolls of the time. She watched her daughter play with paper cutout dolls, pretending that they were teenagers. Ruth felt a doll with breasts would be good for a girl's self-esteem and went on the lookout for a prototype. She first saw the Lilli doll on a trip to Switzerland. Lilli was a blond, fair-skinned doll, complete with hourglass figure and nipples. Ruth thought a toned-down version of the Lilli doll was just what she was looking for. She bought some and took them back to the States to be reproduced.

Handler used the Lilli doll to cast a mold for her new American doll. Sans nipples, the Barbie doll, named after Ruth's daughter Barbara, was introduced to America at a New York toy fair in the winter of 1959. The doll was not an immediate success. Many mothers didn't want to buy a doll with breasts for their daughters and the Sears catalog found Barbie to be "too sexy" to handle.

Barbie's figure *is* a bit outrageous. If she were human-size, her measurements—39-23-33—would be good enough to get her a *Playboy* pictorial. And those legs go on for miles!

Some of you ladies will remember the "Growing Up Skipper" doll that was sold in 1974. With a turn of her arm—voilà—she grew breasts. This may not have been the best message to instill in prepubescent girls, that they would all grow big beautiful breasts. Many wouldn't. Little girls liked the idea, but many parents did not, and complaints forced Mattel to pull the doll from the market.

Is there a dungeon Barbie?

Yes, kind of. A British woman, Susanne Pitt, is marketing a kinky version of the classic Mattel doll. What she does is put the head of "Superstar Barbie" on big-breasted doll bodies of her own making. Some of these "bad Barbies" wore black S&M outfits and were sold on a Web site, until Mattel prosecuted her in New York in 2001. Pitt won the preliminary ruling in November 2002, when Judge Laura Taylor ruled the S&M doll wasn't "a market substitute for Barbie dolls." She noted, somewhat sarcastically, "To the court's knowledge, there is no Mattel line of S&M Barbie." Maybe not, but Mattel *has* introduced a sexier Barbie.

What is Lingerie Barbie?

Maybe taking a cue from the above-mentioned S&M Barbiemaker, Mattel came out with a Lingerie Barbie for Christmas 2002. The virginal girl-next-door has a decidedly new look. This special edition Barbie doll, comes with sexy black or pink garters, silk stockings, stiletto heels, and other various accoutrements. Says Mattel, "Barbie exudes a flirtatious attitude in her heavenly merry widow bustier ensemble accented with intricate lace and matching peekaboo peignoir." The company readily admits that the new Barbie is an adult-oriented toy.

What happened to the Sex on the Beach and the Screaming Orgasm?

Any nightclub regular will recognize the names Sex on the Beach and Screaming Orgasm as popular cocktails. However, one restaurant chain is finding the drinks to be less popular than they could be.

TGI Friday's did a survey of female patrons and found that only sixteen percent had ever ordered a Screaming Orgasm and only twenty-seven percent a Sex on the Beach, although these two drinks score among the highest in their taste test surveys. The problem, they concluded, was that most women were too embarrassed to order the drinks, especially from a waiter or in front of their children. The answer, apparently, was to rename the drinks.

A Sex on the Beach, which contains one part each of Midori, vodka, and Chambord, and two parts orange juice and cranberry juice, will now be called a Summer Sunset. A Screaming Orgasm, consisting of one part each of Kahlua, vodka, Bailey's, and amaretto, and six parts cream, will be called a Coffee Cooler. By the way, the two top cocktails in their taste test were Long Island Iced Tea and strawberry daiquiri.

Are women with PMS worse drivers?

It's an old joke that women don't drive as well as men. Now there appears to be a logical rationale to that assertion. Studies of hospital records show that around fifty percent of the women admitted with traffic-accident-related injuries were having PMS at the time. This is three times higher than would be expected normally. Interviews conducted suggest that these women were feeling particularly aggressive at the time of the wreck. So guys, if your wife's having her moody time of month, you may want to do the driving.

Do gays make the best soldiers?

In today's military, it's "don't ask, don't tell." The American armed services don't really want gays in the military, but they will try to look the other way. Such was not the case in ancient Greece.

The Greeks actually encouraged love between two men and quite often stationed the gay lovers side by side. They felt that such a bond would make their soldiers even braver, in that the lovers would be more willing to die together than to appear cowardly in the other's eyes. Gay soldiers were also thought to be more loyal to the army than their heterosexual counterparts, who had a wife and kids at home to think about.

One of the Greek's best corps of shock troops were the Sacred Band of Thebes, which was comprised of three hundred men, all homosexual pairs. They fought valiantly in battle together for nearly thirty-three years. In 338 B.C., they were defeated by Alexander the Great, at the battle of Chaeronea, where two hundred and fifty-four died, and the other forty-six were taken prisoner.

What women's magazine once lost 75,000 subscribers for publishing educational articles on venereal disease?

In 1906, *Ladies' Home Journal* editor Edward Bok decided that, for the good of American women, he would run a series of articles on how to prevent venereal disease. He recommend the seemingly uncontroversial options of abstinence and chastity. Public outrage over his mentioning of a sexual disease cost him 75,000 subscribers. Women's magazines today thrive on publishing any topic dealing with sex. How things have changed!

What is the "Santa Claus effect"?

Christmas is a happy time, especially for teens in love. It is the time of year when a girl is most likely to finally give her boyfriend that most precious of gifts: her virginity. Sociologists at Mississippi State University have determined that while June is the most common month for teens to have casual sex for the first time, December is the most popular month of the year for serious young couples. Romantic partners are three times as likely to have their first sexual encounter in December than those casually dating. This phenomenon, which the researchers call the "Santa Claus effect," was recently reported in the *Journal of Marriage and Family*. They conclude that the whole Christmas spirit thing plays a key role.

What is the world record for kissing?

There is a type of kiss called "maraichinage," which can last for hours. It originated with the Maraichins, inhabitants of Brittany. In this marathon kiss, the partners explore and caress every nook and cranny of the other's mouth with their tongues. However, this practice is nothing compared to what some people will do to get into *The Guinness Book of World Records*.

On January 28, 2002, Louisa Almodovar and Rich Langly of Vineland, New Jersey, set the record for the longest kiss by staying in a lip lock for thirty hours, fifty-nine minutes, and twenty-seven seconds. What makes the feat so amazing is that not only did the couple have to keep their lips together the whole time, but they also had to do it standing up, with no breaks for eating, drinking, or going to the bathroom. The wearing of diapers was not allowed.

What woman has had the most babies?

According to *The Guinness Book of World Records*, that honor goes to the first wife of Feodor Vassilyev (1707–1782), of Shuya, Russia. This poor woman is reported to have borne sixty-nine children. Over a forty-year period (1725–1765), she had sixteen pairs of twins, seven sets of triplets, and four sets of quadruplets. All but two of her children survived infancy.

Who fathered the most children?

The fathering is the easy part. As you would expect, the number is much higher than for the above mother. Naturally, a guy with several wives and concubines holds this record. Moroccan Emperor Mulai Ismail (1646–1727) kept himself busy. In 1703, he had already fathered 525 sons and 342 daughters. By 1721, the number of sons was up to 700.

How long can pubic hair get?

Evidently, pubic hair, for some, can grow to great lengths. According to *The Illustrated Book of Sexual Records*, one woman had pubic hair that reached down to her knees! Another woman is cited whose hair was so dense and full that it reached halfway up to her navel in front, and several inches up the buttocks in the rear.

Why should you conceive in July?

If you want to have twins, try conceiving in July. According to statistics compiled by AllBaby.com, more American twins are conceived in July than in any other month. Some scientists speculate that the longer hours of daylight in July cause females to secrete more follicle-stimulating hormone, which triggers the release of eggs from the ovaries.

To really increase your odds of having twins, eat more yams. The Yoruba people of Nigeria have the highest percentage of twins per capita. A mainstay of their diet is the yam, which releases an estrogen-like chemical. Of course, you could just wait until you are thirty-five, at which age your chances of giving birth to twins is 1 in 27, as opposed to 1 in 35 when you are younger.

What is a nymphomaniac?

Some people use the term "nymphomaniac" rather loosely when referring to a woman whose sex drive is higher than they deem appropriate. Some men even fantasize about nymphomaniacs. The sad truth is that nymphomania is a psychological disorder where a woman is addicted to sex. She is literally insatiable and the compulsion to have sex renders the act totally mechanical and devoid of any intimacy. The man is treated simply as an object. The quest for new men to sexually conquer can interfere with the woman's daily life and add to the feelings of inadequacy that some believe is the root psychological problem from which these poor individuals suffer.

What popular cracker was invented by a vegetarian who abhorred sex?

Graham crackers are made of graham flour, which is simply whole wheat flour. It was promoted by a nineteenth century Presbyterian minister, Sylvester Graham (1794–1851). He was very active in the temperance movement. Graham felt that eating a healthy diet could cure alcoholism and lead to a more wholesome lifestyle. He traveled throughout the United States preaching the evils of eating meats and fats, which he was sure led to sexual promiscuity. His answer to man's lack of virtue was a diet of vegetables, fruits, and unsifted whole wheat flour in place of white bread. His many followers helped make the use of "graham" flour popular and his legacy lives on today in the form of graham crackers.

Graham felt it best for one's health to limit sexual intercourse to a maximum of twelve times a year. So if you're ever feeling a little horny and want to cleanse your soul, get a box of graham crackers and a glass of milk, and think pious thoughts!

When did extending the middle finger become offensive?

Thrusting out the middle finger or "flipping the bird," is one of our more familiar hand gestures (especially at rush hour). Its popularity extends worldwide and it has been around for a very long time. No one is sure how it originated, but people have been waving their middle fingers at one another since at least 500 B.C. How it originally came to be considered an obscene gesture is open to speculation. One explanation is that, when extended, it somewhat resembles a penis. It is also the longest finger, and as such, the easiest to insert into a vagina.

Slapping the back of the fist with the palm means "fuck you" in Italy and Chile. The same message can be conveyed in the Mediterranean by hitting the biceps and lifting the forearm.

The American "okay" sign is also widely known. But in some countries it is not really *okay*. In Brazil, it is considered obscene. In Colombia, the okay sign is placed over the nose to imply that someone is homosexual.

In Egypt, tapping the ends of the index fingers together, means two people are sleeping together. It can also be used to ask another person to sleep with you.

Almost every gesture has some kind of meaning somewhere in the world, so be careful what you do with your hands when traveling abroad; you may convey the wrong message to someone.

CHAPTER FOURTEEN

The Language of Love

How did the prudish Victorians avoid saying explicit words?

The Victorians were so uptight about sex that they covered up nude statues and paintings. They went so far as to put skirts on tables and pianos to hide *their* legs. Many books were banned and burned. They even came up with a new vocabulary to replace any words they found offensive. The following is a brief list:

Old Word	*New Word*
Legs	Limbs
Chicken breasts	Chicken bosoms
Breasts	The neck
Underwear	Unmentionables
Venereal disease	Social disease
Masturbation	The solitary device
Sex	A connection
Pregnant	Enceinte
Gives birth	Is confined
Cock and bull story	Rooster and male-cow story
Cockroach	Roach

The height of this silliness is presented in a nineteenth-century guide to etiquette that recommends keeping books by female and male writers on separate shelves, unless they are married.

Noah Webster, of dictionary fame, also chimed in on the cleaning up of the English language. His particular target of interest was the Holy Bible. He found even its sacred words a little too racy for his high standards. In 1833 he expunged the words "womb" and "teat" entirely. Words like "fornicate," "harlot," and "whore" were replaced with "lewdness." Men's "stones" became "peculiar members."

What are "breast warts"?

Believe it or not, the German word for "nipple" is "bruzewarze," which translates literally to "breast warts." No one ever said the German language was beautiful. In fact, a Swiss dictionary is encouraging couples to use more romantic words when talking about sex.

Blissful Words was written by relationship counselor Klaus Heer, and has been embraced by a group of German Christians as a romantic thesaurus for amorous couples. Instead of "breast warts," Heer prefers words like "love eyes," "heaven's berries," or "buds" (kind of gives the phrase "this Bud's for you" new meaning). He would like people to find their own erotic vocabulary, and toward that end, he runs seminars where he gets people to look at erotic photos and describe the pictures down to the last detail, using their own special words. Isn't that nice.

What are the origins of some of our other modern sex words?

Cunnilingus—From the Latin *cunnus*, meaning "vulva," and *lingere*, meaning "to lick."

Cunt—From the Latin *cunnus* (vulva).

Fag—The word *faggot* was the Middle English word for "kindling," which was used to start a fire. Some think the word "faggot" as a derogatory term for homosexual men, came from the practice of burning alive those caught engaged in sodomy. In any event, the term was shortened to "fag" by the British in the 1880s, and used as a slang for a burning cigarette. In the early 1900s, some thought cigarette smoking effeminate; hence the use of the word for effeminate men.

Fornication—From the Latin *fornix*, meaning "arch." Roman hookers (*lupae*) conducted business under the arches (*fornices*) of temples, bridges, and the Colosseum.

Fuck—Our favorite, and most versatile word, has been taboo since the sixth century, when the Saxons were thought to have brought the vulgar word *foken* for "to beat against," with them to England.

Hickey—From the 1920s expression "doohickey," meaning "small gadget."

Masturbation—From the Latin word meaning "to pollute oneself."

Penis—Latin for "tail."

Nookie—"Getting nookie" is a cute expression for "getting pussy." The word "nookie" is from the old Scottish word *noke*, which meant "crack or recess." The word wasn't used in the United States until the late 1920s.

Queer—The word was first used as a term for a gay man in *Variety* in 1925.

Tit—the word "tit" was used in Old English as far back as the eleventh century. The Anglo-Saxons used the word only when referring to the nipple, not the entire breast. Earlier than this, it is believed that "tit" probably meant "little," which helps explain why we have a small bird named the "titmouse."

Venereal disease—From the Latin phrase *morbus Veneris*, "the sickness of Venus," (the goddess of love and sex), was first used in the sixteenth century.

How's your Greek?

The Greeks invented a silly yet fascinating soap opera-like mythology that they used to govern their lives. Like any good soap opera, it had plenty of sexual intrigue and deceit. Much of our modern sexual terminology derives from Greek mythology. The following are some of the more interesting examples:

Aphrodisiac—Aphrodite was the Greek goddess of intercourse. Cronos, the son of heaven and earth, castrated his father and threw his testicles into the sea. They floated away in the foam of their own semen. It was from this foam that Aphrodite was born.

Erotic—Aphrodite also had a son, Eros, the god of emotional love. She had another son with Dionysius, named Priapus, who was blessed (or cursed) with a perpetual erection.

Gynecology—The Greeks referred to a woman as *gyne*, or "bearer of children."

Hermaphrodite—Aphrodite had a son with Hermes, the Greek god who was the messenger of the other gods. This son was the androgynous Hermaphroditos, who had the organs of both sexes.

Homosexual—It is from the word *homos*, Greek for "the same" that the term "homosexual" derives, not the Latin *homo*, or "man." It was first coined by German doctor Karl M. Kertbeny in 1869.

Lesbian—The Greek isle of Lesbos was home to the famed poetess Sappho. She ran an "academy" for young ladies and wrote erotic poetry about them. Lesbos became the ancient center of lesbianism.

Orgasm—The word "orgasm" is derived from the Greek word *organ*, which means "to ripen, be lustful." It is akin to the Sanskrit word *urja*, meaning "to sap strength."

Pornography—Comes from the Greek word *porneia*, meaning "the writings of and about prostitutes."

What does the word "gymnasium" have to do with nudity?

The ancient Greeks were not shy about showing off their genitals. Athletic competitions of the time were held in the nude. In fact, the word "gymnasium" is from the Greek *gymnos*, meaning "naked." Many young Greek male athletes tied the foreskin of the penis over the glans to help prevent injury. They referred to this technique as *kynodesme*, or "dog tie."

Who were the Amazon women?

Today when we refer to a woman as an Amazon, we usually think of someone very tall and muscular. The term is usually not meant as a compliment. The word "Amazon" has nothing to do with South America. The Greeks had a legend about a fierce tribe of female warriors that burned their breasts off as girls so that they wouldn't interfere with their handling of a bow and arrow. The Greek word for "breastless" is *amazone*.

What fruit's original name meant "testicle"?

Avocados (*Persea americana*), members of the laurel family, are native to Central America, where local populations have enjoyed them for centuries. Their name is a derivation of the Aztec word for testicle (*ahuacatl*), which they somewhat resemble. The Spaniards twisted this word into *aguacate*, and we know it today as avocado, which is certainly a more appetizing name than the original!

Another food plant with a curious name is vanilla (*Vanilla planifolia*). A member of the orchid family, its name comes from the Latin word *vagina*, because it was thought the vanilla pod looked like a you know what.

What famous mountains are named the "Big Tits"?

Any of you who took high school French should already know this one. Perhaps the two most beautiful peaks in North America are Wyoming's Grand Tetons. Nineteenth-century French trappers were so fond of their beauty that they named them "Grand Tetons," which means "big tits" in French. (These guys must have been out in the wilderness a little too long.) An actress with big tits, Jane Russell, has twin Alaskan peaks named in honor of her most prominent features.

What item of lingerie's name means "don't do housework"?

Nightgowns became popular in the 1500s as a comfortable way for men and women to sleep in the colder climates of Europe. Ladies were bound into their whalebone corsets all day and men were buttoned into their tight-fitting waistcoats. A long unisex frock of wool or velvet, with a fur lining, was just the thing to keep one cozy at night.

During the mid-1700s, there began to be some differentiation between men's and women's nightclothes. In France, the negligee appeared. Distinct from a man's nightgown, it was made of silk or brocade with lace or ruffles, and was tighter-fitting, especially around the waist, in order to show off a woman's femininity. Not just for sleeping, a negligee was also worn for relaxing around the house.

The word "negligee" derives from the Latin *neglegere*, meaning "to neglect," or "not to pick up." Because a women lounging around the house in a negligee was not likely to be picking things up, the name seemed appropriate.

What is the jockstrap named for?

Sure, jocks wear jockstraps, but the word "jock" did not always mean "athlete." The word "jock," as you might assume from the word "jockstrap," was first used as a vulgar English slang for penis. In 1886, a strap that held the penis became known as a jockstrap. Aside from referring to the penis, "jock" also was an English pejorative for a not too bright, undereducated man. It was kind of used like our word "boob" is today.

Where does the term "screwing" come from?

No one can say for sure, but it may have been inspired by swine. Pigs have been kept by humans for thousands of years and their mating habits became well known. Perhaps the most unusual thing about pig sex is the pig's penis. Not only is it a foot and a half long; it's also shaped like a corkscrew! The male pig's spiral penis fits into the corkscrewed vagina of the female. Once he gets it in there, they are literally locked together for the ten minutes or so that it takes to complete the act. The male's repeated orgasms each inject the female with up to a pint of semen!

Who was the first sadist?

Sadism, the derivation of sexual pleasure from inflicting pain on others, is probably as old as humankind. However, it didn't have a name until a French author, the Marquis de Sade (1740–1814), came along. His real name was Count Donatien Alphonse François de Sade, and he was your basic sex pervert.

After marrying into a rich family, he started to indulge himself in his favorite hobby—sexually abusing prostitutes. He was caught and imprisoned several times. Each arrest created a bigger scandal and made him more infamous. He eventually landed in the Bastille, where he began to write novels about sexual perversions. When the Bastille was stormed during the revolution, de Sade was moved to an insane asylum. It wasn't until seventy-five years after his death that his name came to represent this kind of sexual perversion.

Who was the first masochist?

Like sadism, masochism has been around forever, and it's also named after a psychotic novelist. Austrian-born author, Leopold von Sacher-Masoch (1836–1895), was raised on hideous stories of violence, gore, and cruelty told to him by his demented wet nurse, and his harsh, police chief father, who gave him the details of all the local sex crimes. He developed recurring dreams about being sexually tortured by dominating women.

Sacher-Masoch played out his sweaty little dreams with his first wife. Humiliation and pain were his sexual turn-ons. His personal sex life appeared in his novels, most notably in *Venus in Furs*, where he writes of slave-master relationships involving whips, beatings, metal studs, corseting, and anal sex. He, like Sade, was committed to an insane asylum by his second wife. He died there, but not before his name became synonymous with the psychosexual disorder of deriving pleasure from pain.

His name was joined with that of Sade to create the word we use to describe the combination of the two perversions—sadomasochism, or S&M. The term was first coined in 1922.

How did "Calamity Jane" come by her unique nickname?

American frontierswoman "Calamity Jane" was born Martha Jane Canary Burke, the daughter of a prostitute. Jane followed in her mother's footsteps in the world's oldest profession. Not only did she turn tricks, Jane also liked to dress up as a man and visit whores as a customer. Her wild lifestyle is probably what earned her the distinctive nickname Calamity Jane. It is believed that Jane contracted a sexually transmitted disease, which she spread around the American West to those unlucky enough to have sex with her.

What does taking the oath in court have to do with genitals?

Think about the words "testify" and "testimony." Yes, their origins are closely associated with the testicles. Both of these words derive from the Latin *testis*, meaning "witness." We now take an oath with our hand on that most sacred book, the Bible. In ancient times, the testicles were so sacred that they were held to give an oath. They were not released until the testimony was complete. Hence the words "testimony" and "testify." By the way, back then women did not take oaths, except marriage vows.

What rock band is named after a steam-powered dildo?

This band revolutionized pop music with their fusion of rock and jazz. Their sound is smooth, complex, and sophisticated, but their name is not. Donald Fagen and Walter Becker named their musical collaboration—Steely Dan—after the steam-powered dildo in the William Burroughs novel *Naked Lunch*.

What popular genre of music was originally a nickname for sex?

Late-nineteenth-century New Orleans was known as much for its night life as for its music. Born out of the city's nightclubs and brothels was the music that became known as jazz. Etymologists speculate that the musicians of the New Orleans red-light district named their improvisational musical style after their popular nickname for sex.

CHAPTER FIFTEEN

For Better or Worse

Who picks up whom?

In our society, men are thought of as the sexual aggressors who try to woo the women of their choosing. It's a happy little delusion that has persisted for ages. Recent studies of Western courting have suggested the dating reality to be somewhat different than first perceived.

Through observations in singles clubs and other social gathering spots, it appears that women actually initiate contact with men in roughly two-thirds of first encounters. These initial encounters are usually quite subtle—establishing eye contact, making a joke, small talk, or a light touch.

This is about as far as it goes, unless the man gets the hint and reciprocates interest. It is up to him to take things to the next level. He is then, more or less, in the driver's seat and can try to make as much progress as the woman will allow.

The woman, however, has the advantage of knowing just how far she will allow things to go on the first few dates. For the man, it's usually somewhat of a guessing game.

Why is the dinner date so common?

Perhaps no other dating ritual is more universal than the dinner date. A man meets a woman and the first thing that comes into his mind (okay, the second thing) is often, "Hey, let's get some food together." Everyone has to do it at least three times a day anyway, so why not do it with someone you are attracted to?

Almost anywhere you go in the world, people share food as a prelude to sex. It is usually the man who makes the food offering, which is interesting when you consider that if they settle down, it is often the woman's responsibility to prepare it.

Why food? Sex and food have been intimately linked since the beginning of human history. The man was traditionally the hunter and protector. This is a common phenomenon in the animal world as well. Whether human or animal, the offering of food shows the male to be a good provider and a worthy potential mate. However, today's man is often expected to provide much more in the way of material goods than simply food.

Why do fools fall in love?

There is perhaps no more joyous feeling in this world than falling in love, full of unbridled passion and childlike silliness. It's pure euphoria, more potent than the most pleasurable drug.

But what is love? "Love is the drug," to quote the musical philosopher Bryan Ferry. Actually, love is *a* drug. We humans are basically big bags of chemicals, and chemicals control everything we do or feel. Love is no exception.

Scientists have isolated a chemical "excitant"—aminephenyl-ethylamine (PEA)—in the brain that causes euphoria. PEA is like a natural amphetamine. When PEA and other neurochemicals such as dopamine and norepinephrine are released into the brain, we feel stimulated. For some reason, the mere thought of the object of our affection in the cortex (thinking brain) causes the release of amines in the limbic system (emotional brain) and bang, instant pleasure. Nothing, however, lasts forever. The brain eventually gets used to the amines, or lowers their production, and the infatuation begins to wear off.

There are high levels of PEA in chocolate, which is why many people eat it when they are feeling depressed. Some people are so hooked on the PEA high that they move from relationship to relationship to keep the high going.

Why do fools stay together?

Once the amine's effects subside, new chemicals—opiates, like endorphins—come into play. Endorphins are "endrogenous morphines" that give feelings of contentment and lessen pain. They calm us and make us feel at ease with the one we love.

Whose job is it to propose marriage?

A lot has changed in male-female relations over the last thirty years. Women have become the equal of men in many areas, except in one major life-altering action—proposal of marriage. This tradition refuses to die. Even in today's world of the "liberated" woman, eighty-two percent of Americans still feel that it is the man's responsibility to propose. The same percentage of people also think that the man should pay for the first date, while seventy-seven percent say the man should also ask for the first date.

Why do people get married?

If there is one sexual universal, it is marriage. People in every culture on Earth, no matter how advanced or primitive, marry. But why?

Marriage assures the male that the offspring he provides for are really his own. A woman has no such doubt. Upon bearing a child, she can be 100 percent sure that it is hers. The man, however, must keep the woman in a completely monogamous relationship with him to have the same peace of mind. His extracurricular activities do not threaten his lineage, but his wife's virtue must be closely guarded.

What is the average married couple's sex life like?

Many married couples enjoy great sex when newly married, but with time and children, sex can fall into a predictable routine. Innumerable studies have been conducted by universities and women's magazines to help us determine what the "normal" married sex life is like. Here is a sampling of some of these studies (all numbers are very rough estimates):

- Sex with your spouse takes about sixteen minutes, including seduction and foreplay. (Couples that are less familiar take a more leisurely forty minutes.)
- Married couples have intercourse between one and three times a week.
- Sixty percent of couples prefer the missionary position.
- Twenty-five percent like the woman on top.
- Sixty percent do it with the lights off.
- Eighty percent have sex with their spouse exclusively.
- Sixty-six percent have performed a strip tease for their spouse.
- Sixty-six percent have showered together.
- Ninety percent of husbands fantasize about their wives.
- Sixty-six percent of husbands fantasize about their friend's wives.
- Forty percent of husbands fantasize about their secretaries.

How does marriage in other cultures differ from our own?

Ninety percent of Americans get married, most in the conventional American way. There are, however, many different ways of choosing a spouse and consummating the marriage. Our familiar wedding traditions seem rather mundane when compared to some of the more "bizarre" practices of other peoples.

The Cashinhua Indians of Brazil have an interesting courting and mating process. The boy gradually begins sleeping with the girl in her hammock. Once he has been sleeping in her family's home for one year, or she becomes pregnant, the two are considered married. What could be less formal? Some other societies have taken their marriage rituals to the other extreme.

It had been the practice in many old farming communities in Europe, Asia, and North Africa to arrange marriages. These planned marriages helped to form beneficial alliances between families and were usually discussed with the intended first. Sometimes the betrotheds may have never met before the day of the wedding. In India, where arranged marriages still occur, couples view marriage in the opposite way that we do. While we see falling in love as the first step toward marriage, the Indian people view marriage as a way to meet someone to fall in love with, as often does happen in Hindu marriages.

It is reported that some sixty percent of marriages in the world today are still arranged.

How common is polygyny?

Polygyny is the state of having more than one wife. It probably sounds either wonderful or horrible to you, depending on your gener and views on marriage. If you are a man, two wives could give twice the pleasure or twice the misery! If you are a woman, having another wife around could mean your husband neglects you or leaves you alone more often! It's all a matter of perspective. Whether good or bad, polygyny is practiced in over seventy-five percent of the world's societies. (While this is a majority of the societies, it is not a majority of the population.)

In these cultures that permit a man to have more than one wife, only five to ten percent of the men actually do so, usually because it is too expensive. The man is expected to treat his wives equally, and, in many cases, set up separate households for each. Therefore, polygyny is pretty much restricted to the upper classes. Some of history's most powerful leaders were polygynists.

The ancient Chinese and the ancient Hebrews engaged in polygyny. Like the Chinese, Hebrew men enjoyed the company of several wives and concubines. According to the Bible (First Book of Kings), King Solomon at one time had 700 wives and 300 concubines!

Mohammed advocated polygyny to the Islamic faithful to offset the large numbers of men killed in battle and to increase the number of his followers. Islam permitted the taking of up to four wives, or one wife and several concubines. The word "harem" came from the Islamic word for "sanctuary." In it, the women were kept separate, but had to be treated equally. The husband was required to have sex with each of the women on consecutive nights.

The most famous American polygamist was Brigham Young. He had seventeen wives and fathered fifty-six children.

What is polyandry?

We already know what polygyny is: one husband with multiple wives. Polyandry is the opposite arrangement: one wife with multiple husbands. It is much rarer. In fact, only a few cultures practiced this unique marital situation.

The Toda of southern India had a curious custom. When a woman married a man, she also took on all his brothers, even ones that were unborn! Each brother had sexual access to the wife. They all lived in one house and whichever brother was engaged with the wife would leave his walking stick outside the door as a kind of "do not disturb" sign.

The Mongols allowed a woman to marry up to four brothers. One of the brothers had to stay behind if the others were away at war. This ensured the protection of the family.

The opposite arrangement, where a man has the right to marry a woman and her sisters, is called sororate. Usually the eldest sister is married first and the man has an option to marry any others as they come of age. Primitive societies that had such a practice could be found in the Americas, Australia, and Africa.

What is group marriage?

Group marriage, or polygynandry, is a rare arrangement that exists in only a few cultures today, notably the Pahari tribe in north India. Brides cost so much that brothers often have to pool their meager resources to afford one. Later, if they are lucky, they may be able to afford to "buy" another.

The great American experiment in group marriage occurred at the Oneida commune in Oneida, New York, between 1847 and

1881. The commune was founded by the religious fanatic John Humphrey Noyes. His followers were called Perfectionists. Over 500 people lived in the same building. Each had their own room but shared everything else, including their children and sexual partners. Noyes said love for a single person was wrong and forbade a man to ejaculate unless his partner had passed menopause. Copulations could last up to an hour, with the woman having many orgasms. He wanted no births at Oneida, even though everyone was to have sex with everyone else. Young boys were taught sexual techniques, including *coitus reservatus* (the prolonging of erection and delaying of ejaculation) by post-menopausal women. The men were not allowed to ejaculate even after withdrawal and masturbation was forbidden.

In 1867, the birth ban was lifted, but Noyes and his son had claims to all the younger women. Predictably, the other men didn't go for this idea and they revolted. Noyes was forced to flee the commune in 1879.

How common is adultery?

Somewhere between thirty to fifty percent of us (it's hard to get people to freely admit their indiscretions) commit adultery at some time—not a very good commentary on our institution of marriage. Humans are naturally promiscuous, not just in the United States, but in cultures around the globe.

The men of the Italian towns around the Adriatic have made an "institution" out of adultery. Most of the men have a lover they see weekdays, around noon, when their lover's husbands are not at home. Their husbands are in someone else's home! Everybody knows it goes on, but it is forbidden to mention it. Apparently, these lunchtime liaisons are permitted if kept discreet. If exposed, the public humiliation might shatter the family.

Other cultures are more open about their affairs. The Kuikum people, a small tribe in Brazil, slip into the jungle with any of up to twelve different lovers. They, however, are happy to return to the village and openly discuss their exploits. Not to be outdone, the Kofyar of Nigeria can have their male or female lover come to live in their home with them, if they are unhappy with their spouse!

What are trial marriages?

A trial marriage is just that, a marriage that can be backed out of after a period of time if the parties agree (kind of like today's celebrity marriages). Trial time periods varied. Some Germanic societies allowed couples a one-night romantic trial. Tenth-century Anglo-Saxon couples had a seven-year period to try out marriage. The Scottish allowed trial marriages into the 1500s. Other cultures that permitted trial marriages were certain communities of Native Americans, Eskimos, Tibetans, Arabs, and Africans.

What was bundling?

There was a curious form of courtship practiced in Puritan New England. The parents of a prospective bride and groom allowed the potential couple to share a bed for one night. Being Puritan New England, no hanky-panky was permitted. Both would be fully clothed. The girl would either have her dress sewn shut or her legs bound together. A board, known as a bundling board, could be placed between them. After getting to know one another in this restrained fashion and exchanging "sexual energy" for a night, the couple had to decide if they were to be married or not. Bundling remained popular from the 1600s up until the American Revolution.

What were short-term marriage contracts?

A Native American man could enter into a short-term marriage contract with a woman before setting out on a long hunting trip. The woman would accompany him on the outing and perform the duties of a wife, namely cooking and sex. At the end of the hunt, the game would be split between them and the contract terminated.

A similar situation occurred among the forest people of the Congo. A hunter would abduct a bride and take her into the jungle while he hunted. After the woman had bore him a child and weaned it, he would bring her back to the village and give her half the game for the child.

What is wife hospitality?

The height of open adultery can be found among the Inuit Eskimos. In their society it is customary to practice what is known as "wife hospitality," or wife lending. If a male friend or visitor stays at their home, the Inuit husband can ask his wife to have sex with the guest for the length of his stay, which can last for days or even weeks! (And you thought a swimming pool made you popular with friends!) They view this special offering as a form of kinship. Of course, the visitor must reciprocate if the host ever visits him (which he probably will if the guy's wife is attractive). The Zapotec Indians also practice wife hospitality, but they will throw in any unmarried daughter to boot.

What famous Egyptian ruler was married to two of her brothers?

Yes, it was the notorious Cleopatra. Not only did she dally with Marc Antony and Julius Caesar, but she was also married to Ptolemy XII and Ptolemy XIII, her brothers. It was common practice for ancient ruling dynasties to permit incestuous marriages in order to keep the royal bloodlines pure. Cleopatra herself was a sixth-generation offspring of the ruling Greek Ptolemies, who had engaged in incestuous marriages for more than three hundred years.

The Romans also had no problems with incest. Julia Agrippina married her uncle, the emperor Claudius. She is also believed to have had sex with her brother Caligula and her son Nero.

Do married men have less testosterone than bachelors?

There's an old joke about a wife removing her husband's balls once they get married. It seems there may be a little truth to the cliché that men become emasculated by their wives.

Studies have shown that the testosterone levels in monogamous male birds fall after they have found a mate and start taking care of the young. Anthropologist Peter Gray and other researchers at Harvard University wondered if the same phenomenon occurs in human males.

By measuring the testosterone levels in the saliva of a group of single and married men, they found this to be the case. Married men do indeed have less testosterone than their single counterparts, and married men with children have less still. In all men studied, the measured testosterone levels followed the normal cycle of peaking early in the morning and falling off during the day. But the decrease was greater in married men and married fathers.

While researchers don't know the exact reasons for the lowered levels, they suspect it may have evolved to keep fathers from being less hormonally driven. This would help them to remain monogamous and keep the family unit intact.

How do you get a mail order bride?

Originally, it was men settling new areas, such as the American West, who "shopped" for a bride long-distance. Settlers who did not bring a woman with them had few options but to marry a native girl, become homosexual, or "order" a bride. Most times, he had help from his relatives or friends back home in making the arrangements.

Today, "mail order" brides can be found on the Internet. They are primarily foreign women seeking American husbands and citizenship. Most of these women are from Southeast Asia and the former Soviet republics. There are currently over 200 Internet sites featuring some 100,000 to 150,000 of these young ladies. Far from actually being "mail order bride" services, these sites really are comprised of "international singles ads."

Here's the way the process works: You enter one of these sites and scan the girls that the service represents. There are usually color photos of the girls with vital statistics and other pertinent information. For a fee, usually around $200, the service will sell you the girl's address. The rest is up to you and the girl. Generally, correspondence will follow to determine if there is a mutual interest. If so, a meeting can be arranged.

The process gets a little trickier if you want to marry the girl. To bring back a foreign bride, you will have to travel to her country and marry her, or get photos of the two of you together to prove that the two of you really know each other.

With all the American women around, why does a guy go looking for a mail order bride? The allure for the American man is in having his pick of thousands of women and marrying a girl who may be more subservient and loyal than an American woman would be. Most men who marry a foreign mail order bride are much older than the girl, and many feel they can mold their new bride into the "perfect" wife.

So what's in it for the woman? The benefits for the girl are escaping what may be undesirable living conditions in her home country, becoming an American citizen, and marrying a man who may be financially well off. She also will probably have more marital freedom in the United States than she would be accorded in her native culture.

So while marrying a mail order bride whom you barely know may sound kind of dopey to most of us, for some people it's actually a win-win situation.

CHAPTER SIXTEEN

The Human Animal

What are the differences between male and female sex hormones?

Sex hormones are chemicals produced by the ovaries, testicles, and adrenal glands, and secreted directly into the bloodstream. They help determine the sex of a fetus, trigger puberty, control development of the genitals, and exert influence over sexual behavior.

There are two types of sex hormones—androgens and estrogens. Both hormones are present in males and females, but in differing amounts. Men have more testosterone (an androgen) and women have more estrogen.

Estrogen is primarily produced in a woman's ovaries. Aside from stimulating the growth of the breasts, pubic hair, and sex organs at puberty, estrogen also regulates the menstrual cycle. However, it does not seem to have much of an influence on female sex drive.

Androgens, on the other hand, are mainly produced in a man's testes. Small amounts are also made in a woman's ovaries, and in the adrenal glands of both sexes. Androgens control the development of a boy's testicles and penis, the growth of facial and body hair, muscle growth, and deepening of the voice at puberty. The androgen testosterone is responsible for an adult male's sex drive.

Just because women have less testosterone than men doesn't necessarily mean they have a lower sex drive. It is thought that women respond to much smaller levels in their system than men do.

Do we all start out female?

During the first five weeks after conception, a male fetus and a female fetus look about the same. The basic human template from which we are all formed hasn't differentiated the sex organs at this early stage. All embryos have folds of tissue that may develop into a scrotum or labia, raised tissue that can become a penis or clitoris, and tissues inside the embryo that may grow into testicles or ovaries.

If there is a Y-chromosome trigger present from the father, the embryo will begin to develop testicles and make its own testosterone between the fifth and eleventh weeks. The raised tissue will grow into a penis instead of a clitoris and the folds will fuse shut to form the scrotum, instead of splitting open to form the vaginal opening. If this basic human template is not triggered to change by the Y chromosome, the fetus will develop into a girl.

So basically, we all start off programmed to be girls for the first five weeks, but some of us are switched into becoming boys, thanks to dad's Y chromosome. In fact, all men have a small remnant of tissue by the prostate that would have developed into a uterus if we had not been instructed to be male.

Why aren't there more women than men?

If you think about it, why does nature need so many men? (Many women ask themselves this question). If one man produces millions of sperm a day, and only one is needed to fertilize a woman, we really don't need so many guys around, biologically speaking. However, upon deeper reflection, we start to see that from a standpoint of genetic diversity, the more men the better. For example, if the male-to-female ratio was too low, there would be a drastic drop in genetic diversity. This is not a healthy condition for any species, as they would become less likely to be able to adapt to changes in the environment and become more likely to be devastated by disease. So ladies, men really are a necessary evil.

Why is perfume so sexy?

The perfume industry makes billions of dollars a year on our fascination with how we smell. This is no new thing. Man has been producing perfumes for ages. The main motivator for its use has not been hygiene, but sex. Many of the earliest perfumes were made from the sexual scent glands of animals.

Musk is a jelly-like red pheromone (sex hormone) taken from the East Asian musk deer. Civet is another such scent, obtained from secretions of the Ethiopian civet cat, while castoreum is a sexual attractant isolated from beavers. The fact that so many animals communicate sexually through odors belies the concept of smell as a primeval sexual stimulator.

What are our natural perfumes?

We humans, like the animals mentioned above, produce our own special sexual aromas. We are not consciously aware of their powerful effect on us. One such human pheromone is called apocrine. It is produced in some of our favorite erogenous zones—the armpits, groin, and nipples—beginning at puberty. The body hair in these areas acts as a wick to put the pheromones into the air.

It is thought that we humans detect pheromones through the vomeronasal gland found behind the nose. Pheromones detected here can stimulate hormonal responses within the body. A woman's sense of smell is more acute at the time of ovulation. Women have a better sense of smell than men in general, but it is heightened when she is most fertile. This may help her to be more attracted by a man's pheromones when it is most likely for her to conceive.

Tests have shown that women living together may find that their menstrual cycles become synchronized because of pheromones. Some pheromones have a different effect, depending on when one smells them. Androtestosterone, found in male sweat, turns off most women unless they are ovulating, when they find it doesn't bother them so much.

Americans consciously find body odor offensive, unlike some

of our European cousins, so we spend a fortune on perfumes and deodorants. Whether we like body odor or not, one thing is clear. If we like someone, we invariably like the way they smell.

Which smells turn people on?

There is actually an institute that studies such things—the Smell & Taste Treatment and Research Foundation in Chicago. Most of their research centers on the tastes and smells of food. Their studies lead them to realize that many food smells can have an effect on sexual arousal. In 1995, director Alan Hirsch looked into which smells increase blood flow to a man's penis. Not surprisingly, many did. Curiously, the biggest turn-on aroma was a combination of pumpkin pie and lavender. For the ladies, a mixture of Good & Plenty candy and cucumber caused an increased vaginal blood flow, and so did baby powder. Oddly, the smell of Good & Plenty without cucumber, reduced arousal, as did the smell of cherries, barbecue, and, ironically, men's cologne.

They took their tests one step further and learned that women who masturbate frequently were most aroused by a Good & Plenty and banana nut bread mixture. Most multiorgasmic women tested experienced reduced arousal from baby powder. Does any of this make any sense? Probably not. But if you want further clarification, check out Hirsch's book on the subject, *Scentsational Sex*.

Why do women have high-pitched voices?

The obvious answer has to do with the voice box. The average female larynx is about a third smaller than her male counterpart's. Thus, a woman's vocal cords are shorter and their voices are usually about an octave higher.

So what is the sexual significance of this difference? The theory goes that the higher pitch of the female voice is more childlike and thus, subconsciously, brings out the paternal instincts in the male to protect the female and her offspring. That is not to say that some men don't find deep, throaty female voices sexy.

Why do men have external genitals?

One reason that men's testicles hang outside the body cavity is to lower their temperature, and thus help increase the number and motility of the sperm produced. Another advantage to external male genitals, one that is considered by some scholars to be even more important, has to do with human locomotion. A study of mammal species reported in the *Journal of Zoology* found that those species with a "concussive" type of movement (deer, kangaroos, monkeys, horses, etc.) tend to have their testicles on the outside, while those with a gentler form of locomotion (sloths, manatees, elephants, moles, etc.) keep them inside the body. Animals that run or jump, like early man did, need to protect their testicles from the pressures that are exerted on them during vigorous activity. Running or jumping too hard applies pressure to the abdomen and squeezes internal testicles. Since the human reproductive tract has no sphincter, such squeezing would expel the sperm and waste it. By having the testicles hanging between the legs, nature has eliminated this problem, but exposed them to other sorts of physical dangers.

Why do we mate face-to-face?

Of all the numerous possible sexual positions, by and large, humans around the world prefer the good old missionary position. Our face-to-face mating is one of the things that sets humans apart from the animal world. With rare exception, we humans are the only animals to mate face-to-face. (The two-toed sloths mate vertically while hanging by their arms from a tree branch, and the bonono have also been observed mating face-to-face in captivity).

Women, unlike other primates, have vaginas that are angled downward. Without a downward-oriented vagina, face-to-face intercourse would be very uncomfortable. The other primates have backward-pointed vulvas, and thus do it from behind. Our face-to-face mating habit leads to greater pair bonding, with the result that "making love" is more of a spiritual matter than simply an animal-like function.

By the way, it was St. Augustine who decided that face-to-face intercourse with the man on top was the only acceptable way to do it. Augustine was a fourth-century Roman who lived the wild life until he converted to Christianity. Then he decided no one else should have fun. He tried to standardize sex for the Christian world. He saw sex as a necessary evil, but said it should only be engaged in for procreation, done in the "missionary position." We call it the missionary position because early Christian missionaries, who were appalled by native peoples doing it "doggy-style," insisted that they also mate face-to-face, with the woman on the bottom.

Why do women have fleshy breasts?

Look around the animal kingdom. You won't find a mammal that has enlarged breasts, unless they are producing milk to feed their young. Sure, their nipples are always present, but the breasts are enlarged only while fulfilling their function of nourishing offspring. Why is the female human so well-endowed throughout adult life?

According to Desmond Morris, author of *The Naked Ape*, when humankind began to walk erect, there were some fundamental changes in the presentation of the sexual structures. As we moved away from the rest of the primates on the evolutionary tree, not only did we lose most of our primate ancestor's hair, but the female body parts that attracted the male primates were also reoriented forward and upward.

Most primates copulate with the male entering from behind. Therefore, the female ape's buttocks are presented to the male as a sexual attractant. Walking around on all fours, the rear end was the most visible place for this sexually attractive body structure to be located. However, when humans stood up and walked on two legs, the front of the body, which faces those we are communicating with, would be a more strategic place for the parts to move. The ornaments of the primate rear end (i.e. buttocks and vulval lips) thus evolved to the front of the female.

A woman's vulva is obviously toward the front today, but what about the buttocks? They are still on the hind end. Instead of a shifting forward of the buttocks, what Morris believes actually happened was that the breasts became enlarged to mimic the fleshy primate behind. He also theorizes that a woman's red, full lips around the mouth evolved to mimic the vulva.

The theory goes that females with bigger breasts and fuller lips attracted more males than the others, and thus bred more. Over the eons, these traits were enhanced to yield the condition we are familiar with today.

Big breasts also serve the more functional purpose as storehouses of fat for lactation and nutrients during times of hardship. Breasts are primarily made up of fat. For this reason, you don't see many skinny women with big bosoms, unless they have been artificially augmented.

While big breasts are worshiped by some today, they did have some evolutionary drawbacks. Among their major drawbacks, they tended to flop about while running, obstructed the woman's view while bending to gather food, could suffocate an infant, and are quite sensitive.

Why does man have such a large penis?

Man has the biggest penis size relative to body size of all the primates. There is no real biological reason why the male human penis has to have such prodigious length and girth. A thinner penis would inseminate females just as well. It is thought that human males evolved large-size penises because the human female liked them so much. By mating with well-hung males, the females unwittingly helped to selectively breed men with big members. Over the course of evolution, the big penis won out, much to the enjoyment of women.

Why do men have facial hair?

No one immediately apparent physical feature says "man" more than does facial hair. But why do men have facial hair, and women don't? Male facial hair seems to serve no other useful purpose than to highlight the sex of an individual. Facial hair has an indeterminate form of growth, meaning it will keep on growing if not trimmed. A beard will grow at the rate of about six inches a year if uncut. Since facial hair doesn't appear until a boy goes through puberty, it is basically a form of sexual display. Women, even at a great distance away, can tell a person with full facial hair is a man.

The record for male beard growth is seventeen-and-a-half feet by a Norwegian named Hans Langseth. The moustache record belongs to an Indian, Kalyan Ramji, who took twenty years to grow his eleven-foot handlebars.

Why do we have pubic hair?

Over the millions of years of evolution, we humans have lost the total covering of body hair that our primate ancestors retained. We didn't exactly "lose" our hair, though. We still have as many hair follicles as do the apes. It's just that it doesn't grow much, except in certain rather strategic places.

One theory as to the retention of pubic hair is that it acts as a dry lubricant, to reduce skin friction during all of the action of intercourse. (Nasty place for a blister, the pubic region.) Another possible reason for pubic and underarm hair is that these hairs help to produce sweat and retain sexually stimulating odors.

So why then do men have hairier faces and chests than women? Desmond Morris speculates that women lack hair around the lips and breasts to make these areas more sensitive to touch and thus sexual stimulation. Men don't seem to need any more sexual stimulation than they already possess.

CHAPTER SEVENTEEN

The Birds and the Bees

Why do pigs need vibrators?

People enjoy vibrators, so why not pigs? This is the thinking of a Dutch company marketing a vibrator for pigs. Obviously the pigs can't use the device for their own pleasure. The contraption is used to artificially inseminate sows. It was found that a sexually aroused sow is more receptive to being inseminated. The Schippers Company has come up with the MS Reflexator, which is a vibrator hooked up to a sperm reservoir. Now the pigs are happier and so are the pig farmers.

What is "penis captivus"?

There is a phenomenon in the canine world known as "penis captivus." When a male dog is copulating, a knotlike structure forms on the end of his penis, effectively locking it inside the bitch's vagina until after ejaculation, which may take a good ten minutes. Contrary to what some people believe, penis captivus is not really possible in humans.

What is a hermaphrodite?

Some forms of life, such as earthworms and many plants, are hermaphrodites that can self-fertilize. (Most of these species, however, prefer to outbreed.) Hermaphrodites have male and female reproductive structures.

Some animals are transsexual and can change from one sex to another as needed. The cleaner fish of the Great Barrier Reef live in groups of one male to every five or six females. If the male dies, the dominant female will metamorphose into a male.

How do porcupines make love?

The answer to this old joke is "very carefully," which is indeed the case. Porcupine sex is somewhat bizarre. The male gets an erection and stands up on his hind legs, some six feet away from the female, and proceeds to urinate on her. (Yes, porcupines can urinate with an erection, even though people can't.) As you may imagine, this golden shower tends to provoke and agitate the female, who snarls and snaps at him. He then approaches her, usually on three paws, while stroking his penis with the fourth. Now comes the tricky part. He must mount her from the rear, but only if she folds down all her back quills. If all goes well, he thrusts into her. Some young, inexperienced female porcupines may not fold down all the quills, or forget to move the barbed tail out of the way. This complicates matters and can be quite a pain for the male.

Did the dinosaurs have penises?

Yes, the big guys had sex, too. Curiously, though, the dinosaurs had no penises. They had long bones (the original boner) to maneuver the male sex organ (the cloacca) into place. *Tyrannosaurus rex* had an eight-to-ten-inch bone, while the *Brontosaurus's* bone was a foot and a half long. The cloacca was set back beneath the tail, as in birds today. (Yes, the birds really did evolve from the dinosaurs.) Another sexual trait that the dinosaurs are thought to have had in common with birds were their vibrant colors. Male birds use their bright coloration to attract a mate. The dinosaurs probably did, too. Some scientists also speculate that the dinosaur's huge horns and spikes were used more for sexual displays and rutting than for attack or defense, similar to the elk and bighorn rams of today.

Do animals have orgasms?

The poor animals; sex in their world is a mechanical exercise that holds no pleasure for the female. Women are the only female animals that are known to experience an orgasm, although some ferrets and rabbits may also achieve this end. Animals have sex for one reason—reproduction. Therefore, female animals are only receptive to the male's advances when they are in heat, which may be only once a year. Human females evolved to be fertile year-round and receptive to sex anytime they please.

Being fertile year-round was a good evolutionary reproductive strategy, in that it ensures an even distribution of babies throughout the year, raising their chances of survival. Animals that bear all their young at the same time risk the loss of an entire generation if environmental conditions are adverse or resources become limited. So not only is human sex fun, but it is also evolutionarily advantageous. We have the best of both worlds.

What animal copulates the longest?

Snakes take the most time to copulate. They have two penises, called "hemipenes," one on each side of the body. Each penis has backward-facing barbs at the base, allowing the male snake to lock into the female for periods ranging from eight to twelve hours. He can use either penis, depending on which side the female snake is on. The longest recorded snake union was one of nearly twenty-three hours between two rattlesnakes. Once the female snake has acquired the sperm, she can store it in her body for several years until needed.

At the opposite end of the spectrum, mosquitoes, who do it in mid-flight, copulate in about two seconds (slightly shorter than some men you may know!).

What animal has the largest sperm?

A sperm whale, perhaps, or an elephant, or a hippopotamus? Sorry. You might not believe this, but the lowly fruit fly is the sperm champ!

While not all species of fruit fly produce large sperm (most produce "normal" small sperm), the *Drosophila hydei* produces sperm up to two-thirds of an inch in length. This is an amazing 300 times larger than human sperm! The fly itself is only about a tenth of an inch long. In order to fit within the fly, the sperm is balled up like a mess of spaghetti.

The reproductive advantage to making lots of small sperm is quite obvious: increased chance of successful fertilization. *Drosophila hydei*, however, only produces a measly 250 or so sperm. What is the reason for this? Apparently these large sperm have up to an eighty percent success rate. We humans produce millions of sperm at a time and usually none of them is successful.

The male fly's sperm are deposited into a sperm storage chamber in the female. As the female's egg passes the chamber entrance, a sperm is pulled into the egg. Unlike in many other animals, where only the head of the sperm is embedded into the egg, the fly's sperm is sucked into the egg in whole. The necessary DNA is only found in the sperm head, so the purpose of the tail being engulfed is unknown. It is believed that the tail may serve as an energy source for the developing embryo.

By the way, if you guessed that the hippo had the largest sperm, you were way off the mark. The hippopotamus produces the smallest sperm in the animal kingdom!

Which animals copulate the most?

You may have heard the expression "fuck like rabbits." It turns out that the rodent species do go at it more frequently than other species. Certain hamsters and gerbils can copulate 100 times an hour. There seems to be no wearing these little critters out.

Which animal has the most nipples?

The answer is an animal you've probably never heard of: the tenrac (*Centetes ecaudatus*). Of all the 18,000 mammal species, this insect-eating, hedgehog-like creature from Madagascar has twenty-two or twenty-four nipples.

What is a dork?

No, not your boss! This pejorative is really the accepted name of a whale's penis. And it's no ordinary penis. The whales, as you might imagine, have the world's largest penises. The blue whale is the champ, with a ten-foot-long member that is one foot in diameter. African bull elephants have nothing to be ashamed of either. They are the land-animal champs, coming in at five- to six-foot-long penises.

Which animal has the biggest testicles?

It would seem to follow that the species with the largest penises would also have the largest testicles, and this is indeed the case. The African elephant is the land champ again, with balls weighing in at 4.4 pounds each. The northern right whale (*Eubalaena glacialis*) is the overall king; a pair of these testicles can weigh up to 2,200 pounds! That's a lot of semen.

Why do storks bring babies?

Okay, they don't bring babies. But for years this is what parents told their children to avoid having to tell them the embarrassing truth. But of all animals to have deliver a baby, why the stork?

This legend started in Germany and Sweden long ago. Every spring, white storks return to Europe from their wintering grounds in Africa. Upon their return, the storks seek out suitable nesting sites to raise their young. Frequently, they build their large nests high up on chimneys or rooftops. Since the storks returned every spring, the residents thought that they brought good luck and fertility for the occupants of the home the stork chose.

To avoid telling their children the facts of life, parents would tell them that the stork delivers babies, and that the mother needed bed rest after the baby was delivered because she was bitten by the stork. Today, with the advent of UPS and FedEx, that story just doesn't fly!

What are some bizarre facts about animal sex?

- The shovel-shaped penis of the dragonfly scoops out the sperm of other suitors.
- Porpoises enjoy group sex.
- Wild animals, as a rule, don't get VD, although otters can get herpes.
- The sperm of a mouse is longer than the sperm of an elephant.
- Koalas, iguanas, and Komodo dragons all have forked penises (split in two).
- The rhinoceros penis is two feet long.
- The mosquito penis is one one-hundredth inch.
- The raccoon penis has a little bone in it that has been used as a toothpick by some.
- The poor male penguin has only one ejaculation a year.
- Minks fornicate for up to eight hours at a time.
- Chimpanzees spend no time with foreplay, averaging about three seconds per copulation.
- Hamsters can have sex seventy-five times a day.
- Shaw's jird (a desert rat) holds the record for frequency of copulation—up to 224 times in two hours!
- The majority of giraffes and turkeys are bisexual.
- A gorilla's penis is a mere two inches long.
- Like humans, fish practice fellatio.
- The six-inch-long Alpine banana slug has a thirty-two inch penis.
- Beavers and hamsters will, on occasion, mate face-to-face.
- Most male birds don't have a penis, but rather holes that pass the sperm to the female.
- When a male deer rubs his antlers on a tree, it is a form of masturbation.